Prophecy Power

Strength from God to Face Your Future

by Terry James

Contents

Introduction 3

1—Powering Up for Supernatural Battle 5

2—The Power-Filled Sentry 14

3—Scoffers and Scoundrels 26

4—Overpowering These Perilous Times 37

5—Rapture Readiness 49

6—Planet Earth Throws a Party! 61

7—This Is Your Life! 72

8—Party's Over! 83

9—Hell on Earth 94

10—Christ's Return, Reign, and Restoration 105

11—God's Great Prophecy Power on Display 116

12—The Prophecy Power-Filled Life (Part 1) 126

13—The Prophecy Power-Filled Life (Part 2) 138

Answers to For Additional Study Questions 149

Cover Image © 1996 PhotoDisc, Inc.

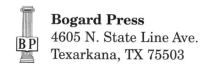
Bogard Press
4605 N. State Line Ave.
Texarkana, TX 75503

Fellowship Bible Study Series

Prophecy Power
Strength from God to Face Your Future
by Terry James

© Bogard Press 2004

Series Editor, Kyle Elkins
Editor in Chief, Larry E. Clements

4605 N. State Line Ave.
Texarkana, TX 75503

Phone: 1-800-264-2482
www.abaptist.org

1060413

ISBN 0892113553

Printed in the United States of America.

Introduction

Key Prophecy Power Truth

"the testimony of Jesus is the spirit of prophecy"
(Rev. 19:10).

Foreknowledge Is Power

Philosophers and educators have long proclaimed that knowledge is power. God's Word, the Bible, proves by fulfilled prophecies throughout the ages that foreknowledge is infinite power!

To intimately know Jesus Christ is to have a personal relationship with the only source from which knowledge of future things comes. When we are born again into the family of God, we tap instantly into that fountain of life that will never end, and into God's omniscient (all-knowing) power to understand, with 100 percent soul-satisfying reassurance, that ours is a brilliant destiny. God's Word tells the soul-empowering truth about Bible prophecy. Jesus is at the center of eternal matters.

No Fear

You need not fear what the future might hold for you and those you love. You can know—beyond any doubt—the causes and reasons for the troubling events and unsettling issues of everyday life unraveling all around you. More than that, by understanding your heavenly Father's plans for your future, through study of His prophetic Word you can live in freedom beyond any liberty available to those who haven't made Jesus their Lord. The promise comes directly from the Lord Jesus Christ: "If the Son therefore shall make you free, ye shall be free indeed" (John 8:36).

The Apostle Paul expanded on the great truth that there is liberty in Christ. "For God hath not given us the spirit of fear; but of power, and of love, and of a sound mind" (2 Tim. 1:7). Jesus is the One who takes away all fear and makes us truly free. This is godly empowerment for the Christian.

Jesus Revealed

The last book in the Bible, the Revelation, is not the revelation of the many judgments to be found throughout its text. It is the Revelation, or the "unveiling," of a Person. Too often preachers, teachers, and those who sit in the pews and classrooms of churches in this last time think of and present Jesus as the tiny baby wrapped in swaddling clothes. They more often than not look at Him as the pathetic figure hanging on that cruel Roman cross. The more spiritually attuned even see Him as the resurrected and ascended Christ who appeared to many after arising from the dead. But fewer and fewer these days consider Him as the returning King—the theme of the Revelation. You see, He didn't stay that tiny baby in the manger. He grew to perform miracles, to teach and preach the kingdom of God, to offer Himself as the prophesied, once-and-for-all sacrifice for remission of sin—to prove Himself the grace-gift from His Father in Heaven to lost mankind. He didn't stay on that cross or stay buried in the borrowed tomb of Joseph of Arimathea.

Jesus Our Mediator

Neither did He stay on planet Earth as the resurrected Christ in His glorified body, but He returned to the Father's right hand, where He is the one and only mediator between God and mankind (1 Tim. 2:5).

King of all kings!

The Book of Revelation, we as Christians must understand, is the revealing, the unveiling, of the Lord Jesus in all His majesty, power and glory. He is coming back to put down all who oppose God's holy will. He is the King of all kings and Lord of all lords!

Supernatural Power

When Christians tap into the truth of the power that is in their mighty Jesus—really know Him and who He is in the fullness of His glory—their lives grow in empowerment from on high—from the very throne of the Living God! God empowers His children for their missions on His behalf, as He did for His Son's earliest disciples. Jesus said, "And, behold, I send the promise of my Father upon you: but tarry ye in the city of Jerusalem, until ye be endued with power from on high" (Luke 24:49).

Power To Change

Prophecy is not in the Bible to thrill and sensationalize. The prophetic Word isn't given to merely satisfy curiosity about the future. It is a dynamic tool that edifies the Christian who studies it. It is a powerful instrument for evangelism. Prophecy is there to change lives—the lives of the ones who study and meditate upon the prophetic Word and the ones whose lives the students of prophecy touch as they carry out the Lord's Great Commission. "Go ye therefore, and teach all nations, baptizing them in the name of the Father, and of the Son, and of the Holy Ghost: Teaching them to observe all things whatsoever I have commanded you: and, lo, I am with you alway, even unto the end of the world. Amen" (Matt. 28:19, 20).

A Brilliant Destiny

Bible prophecy is not gloom and doom; it's just the opposite! Prophecy is God's telling us that no matter how dark the horizon of our perilous times look, we are approaching a time bursting with brilliant, eternal light and pleasures beyond any it is within our ability to imagine: "But as it is written, Eye hath not seen, nor ear heard, neither have entered into the heart of man, the things which God hath prepared for them that love him" (1 Cor. 2:9).

Just turn to the back of the Book containing the greatest story ever told. We win! Make the study of Bible prophecy an indispensable part of your life daily. Feel God's strength to face your future flow into your soul while you pray, read and meditate upon the whole Word of God. Experience the infinite power of your awesome God energize you for these exciting days in which we have been given the privilege of living for Him.

Powering Up for Supernatural Battle

Soldiers of ancient Roman times got ready for battle by putting on metal plates that covered the parts of their bodies most vital to life. Medieval knights went even further by wearing metal suits that covered their entire bodies. Modern knights who must engage in war often wear special protection, and it is reported that future warriors will be outfitted with fully powered bionic and robotic body armor that is offensive as well as defensive in capability.

In more relevant terms for us today, football players suit up with the latest fiberglass and plastic armor when preparing to clash with their foes on their green and white-striped fields of battle. What is relevant to us as Christians here is that we are in a contest—a war—more super than a Super Bowl. In truth, we are in a supernatural arena of conflict.

Ancient Enemy, Modern Foe

Paul the Apostle describes the foes Christians face in this "Supernatural Bowl." "For we wrestle not against flesh and blood, but against principalities, against powers, against the rulers of the darkness of this world, against spiritual wickedness in high places" (Eph. 6:12).

"Know your enemy" is the number one rule for planning battle strategy. Generals and football coaches alike know that you must find and exploit the foe's most vulnerable point. Satan is a seasoned and savvy general in the war against Christians. He knows that many seminaries, preachers, teachers and individual Christians have become weakened because of lack of study, prayer, and meditation concerning the Bible. He knows we, as a whole, have particularly refused to delve into God's prophetic Word.

Dangerously Dumb

God, through the prophet Hosea, spoke to Israel of the danger in neglecting His divine instructions for conducting the ongoing war against their supernatural enemy. Be assured, it's the same enemy we as Christians face today: "My people are destroyed for lack of knowledge" (Hosea 4: 6).

Apathy Abounds

Satan is using our lack of knowledge to bring about apathy within Christ's body, the Lord's churches. That lack of concern, if not reversed, might result in millions of lost people dying apart from God—or moving into the era of Tribulation—the seventieth week prophesied by Daniel the prophet in Daniel 9:24-27 (which we will study later).

Spiritually Spearing Satan

The devil obviously has studied in-depth Christians' lack of interest in prophecy. It's high time that we begin scouting him for a change. We can best do so by considering the evil one's plans for the world. We can learn his treacherous plan for mankind through the power of the Prophetic Word of God. In big-picture terms, his endgame is laid out in prophecy. Only the details of his plans reside in the hazy mist of history yet future. That's where examining current events and issues under the microscope and light of the prophetic Word will empower us to conduct ourselves as spiritual warriors. For, it is indeed all-out spiritual warfare that confronts us!

Suiting up for Spiritual Warfare

Paul tells us in the following verses the type of spiritual armor we must put on to compete and become victorious against the worst of all enemies: "Wherefore take unto you the whole armour of God, that ye may be able to withstand in the evil day, and having done all, to stand. Stand therefore, having your loins girt about with truth, and having on the breastplate of righteousness; And your feet shod with the preparation of the gospel of peace; Above all, taking the shield of faith, wherewith ye shall be able to quench all the fiery darts of the wicked. And take the helmet of salvation, and the sword of the Spirit, which is the word of God: Praying always with all prayer and supplication in the Spirit, and watching thereunto with all perseverance and supplication for all saints" (Eph. 6:13-18).

Our Supernatural Sword

The "whole armour of God" is wrapped up in one Word: "Jesus." John, in his gospel account, says: "In the beginning was the Word, and the Word was with God, and the Word was God" (John 1:1). The entire Word of God comes to its full unveiling with the Revelation of Jesus Christ, the last of the 66 books of the Bible. There is shown the astonishing power of Christ's words. "And out of his mouth goeth a sharp sword, that with it 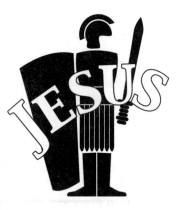 he should smite the nations: and he shall rule them with a rod of iron: and he treadeth the winepress of the fierceness and wrath of Almighty God" (Rev. 19:15).

Prophecy tells us that Christ's Word is an all-powerful sword that will give victory over our foes: sin, Satan, and the devil's hordes. It is time for Christian pastors, teachers, and students to dress for the supernatural end-time battle that is upon us.

Powerful Thrust of Prophecy

This study will show that the prophetic Word is vital to Christian growth and to living a Spirit-filled, joyful, thus God-empowered life rather than a life fearful of what the future holds. Prophecy is almost one-third of the whole Word of God. Nearly 400 of the 1,189 chapters in the Bible are prophetic in nature. How senseless—even tragic—it is to neglect this pow-erful spiritual sword God has given us, with which He expects us to victoriously oppose the soul-destroying enemy we face.

By ignoring or refusing to study Bible prophecy, we are telling Jesus, "We don't believe your words when you say, 'These things I have spoken unto you, that in me ye might have peace. In the world ye shall have tribulation: but be of good cheer; I have overcome the world' (John 16:33)."

Why Study Prophecy?

Not convinced yet that it's vital, as a Christian, to study Bible prophecy? Let's go over some scriptural reasons God so graciously provided information about things to come for His children who obediently seek His Truth.

Prophecy Defined

- Nearly one-third of the Bible is prophetic. One-half of that has been fulfilled; the other half is in the process of preparation for fulfillment. We will learn details about this stage setting for end-time prophecy during this study.

- The gift of prophecy is a twofold gift, according to God's Word.

  1. Prophecy is "forthtelling." The gift of prophecy as defined as "forthtelling" has to do with speaking through Holy Spirit discernment to a current event or situation (Rom. 12:6). "Forthtelling" is not the ability to predict a future event through supernatural power. Some today want to equate this with something they call "word of knowledge," but this error steps well beyond the meaning

of "forthtelling." More often than not, the thing labeled "word of knowledge" is used to glorify the person who purportedly receives and then "forthtells," rather than glorifying God. An example of true "forthtelling" is found in Paul's use of this form of prophesying in 1 Corinthians 1:11; 3:1; and 5:1.

2. Prophecy is "foretelling." Prophecy in this sense is the way we usually think of it. "Foretelling" is divinely inspired speaking with 100 percent accuracy about an event that will take place in the future. We see this form of prophesying in many places throughout the Bible. The prophet Daniel, for example, prophesied through Nebuchadnezzar's dream-vision and his own dream-vision four great kingdoms that would come upon the earth before Christ's return. These kingdoms are now history, with the final form Daniel prophesied to grow out of the fourth kingdom yet to come—the kingdom that Antichrist will rule. (See Daniel, chapters 2, 7—9.)

Specific Reasons to Study Prophecy
- So that you will not be ignorant concerning God's program for the future (1 Thess. 4:13).
- Because God wants you to know His prophetic plan (Psalm 25:14; Dan. 2:28; Amos 3:7; Matt. 11:25; Luke 8:10; Rev. 1:1).
- So we can comfort and encourage each other with the truth that history, for the Christian, has a joyous ending (1 Thess. 4:14; Rev. 21:1-4).
- Because Bible prophecy will challenge us to live godly lives (2 Peter 3:11).

Facts About Bible Prophecy
- Again, approximately 27% of the Bible is prophecy. About one-half of that has been fulfilled. The other half, just over 13%, will be fulfilled as surely as was the previous prophecies.
- Human history and its perplexing twists and turns can be understood only through knowledge of Bible prophecy. Prophecy proves that God is in complete control of histo-

ry—past, present, and future! About this, God says through Isaiah the prophet: "Remember the former things of old: for I am God, and there is none else; I am God, and there is none like me, Declaring the end from the beginning, and from ancient times the things that are not yet done, saying, My counsel shall stand, and I will do all my pleasure: Calling a ravenous bird from the east, the man that executeth my counsel from a far country: yea, I have spoken it, I will also bring it to pass; I have purposed it, I will also do it" (Isa. 46:9-11).

Isaiah says further: "The LORD of hosts hath sworn, saying, Surely as I have thought, so shall it come to pass; and as I have purposed, so shall it stand: This is the purpose that is purposed upon the whole earth: and this is the hand that is stretched out upon all the nations. For the LORD of hosts hath purposed, and who shall disannul it? and his hand is stretched out, and who shall turn it back?" (Isa. 14:24, 26, 27).

- It is impossible to understand the madness and rage against the nation of Israel today, apart from knowing Bible prophecy. The terrorism, the hatred and the reasons God's chosen nation is becoming more and more viewed as the cause of the problems in the Middle East rather than a victim of atrocities can truly be understood only by the spiritually attuned student of biblical prophecy. God's Word says to Israel through Moses, the Lord's chosen deliverer: "For thou art an holy people unto the LORD thy God: the LORD thy God hath chosen thee to be a special people unto himself, above all people that are upon the face of the

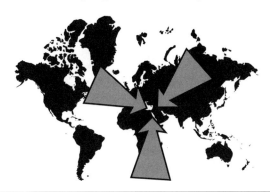

earth" (Deut. 7:6). Israel's great King David spoke to God, confirming truth about the Lord's eternal commitment to that nation: "For thou hast confirmed to thyself thy people Israel to be a people unto thee for ever: and thou, LORD, art become their God" (2 Sam. 7:24).

Requirements for Understanding Prophecy

- The student of prophecy must know Jesus as Savior (be born again) (Dan. 12:8-10; Matt. 11:25; 13:10, 11). Without God the Holy Spirit dwelling within, people are in darkness. They are as dead in God's view. They can know nothing about God's truth, including prophetic truth. They must be born again, as Jesus told one man lost in sin: "Marvel not that I said unto thee, Ye must be born again" (John 3:7).
- The person must know Jesus as Lord (be Holy Spirit-controlled) (1 Cor. 3:1-3; Heb. 5:11-14; 1 John 2:9-11).

The great minds of history have tried to understand where the world is headed. They continue to do so. Will there be war or peace? Will there be a utopian world of happiness and plenty—or will it all end in a cataclysmic thermonuclear holocaust? World diplomats haven't a clue. But the Christian who reads, studies and prays for discernment from the prophetic Word of God about where we stand on God's prophetic timeline is empowered to know the answers to these troubling questions. Such students of Bible prophecy—under the direction of the Holy Spirit—can understand things to come in a way the most learned Ph.D. who is in spiritual darkness cannot.

For Additional Study

1. Who is at the center of all Bible prophecy?

2. What can Bible prophecy do for the believer?

3. What is the number 1 rule for preparing for spiritual battle?

4. What is the Sword of the Spirit?

5. Approximately how much of the Bible contains prophecy?

6. What are the two words that define Bible prophecy?

7. Define each.

8. Give 4 reasons why we should study Bible prophecy.

The Power-Filled Sentry

KEY PROPHECY POWER TRUTH

"And what I say unto you I say unto all, Watch."
Mark 13:37

Local, national, and international news bombard our eyes and ears hourly. We've all heard or even asked the question ourselves: "What's going to happen next?" We live in a world that seems on the verge of insanity. Yet, that impending madness somehow is now so familiar that it almost has become the norm. When we hear of even the most bizarre conduct by people these days, we might be shocked for a second or two. Then it's back to business as usual.

Jesus said that it would be just such a time when He would come back to surprise most everyone. The Lord said, "Therefore be ye also ready: for in such an hour as ye think not the Son of man cometh" (Matt. 24:44).

Troublesome Generation

Jesus also had something to say about the generation alive at the very end of the age. He said: "And as it was in the days of Noe, so shall it be also in the days of the Son of man. They did eat, they drank, they married wives, they were given in marriage, until the day that Noe entered into the ark, and the flood came, and destroyed them all. Likewise also as it was in the days of Lot; they did eat, they drank, they bought, they sold, they planted, they builded; But the same day that Lot went out of Sodom it rained fire and brimstone from heaven, and destroyed them all" (Luke 17:26-29).

Eerily Familiar?

The question we are wise to ask is: "Could ours be the time of which Jesus spoke?"

The days of Noah and of Lot, Jesus said, were times when business at every level of society was going smoothly for the most part. People were getting married, having babies, raising crops, building homes and doing every other kind of construction. They were selling and buying merchandise. They hadn't a clue their worlds were about to be disrupted by great cataclysms.

Societies and cultures, at the same time, suffered every form of crime and perversion, the Book of Genesis tells us. Violence, as a matter of fact, filled the whole Earth. Men's hearts (minds) were fixed on evil continually, the Word of God says.

What About Us?

Have you watched sitcoms lately? Have you scanned your e-mail and been deluged with pornography? Have you heard the foul language with the blasphemous use of God's name often at its core? Have you been a witness to road rage, or taken part in it? Have you observed life around you in general? Do we fit Paul's prophetic prediction for the perilous times of the last days in 2 Timothy 3? Are we "lovers of pleasures, more than lovers of God?"

We can't know the number of people alive on Earth at the time of Noah's Flood or during the time of Sodom and Gomorrah's catastrophic judgments, but it's reasonable to wonder if, there might not be about the same ratio of lost to saved people as are in our time.

Noah and seven of his family members were all who escaped the Flood. God couldn't find even ten people righteous in His eyes during the moments just before He removed Lot from the doomed area.

Hard of Hearing

Just like Noah, who preached repentance for 120 years following the time God told him He would destroy the world with water, true preachers and teachers of God's gospel message have for many centuries been preaching and teaching to a rebellious world of Earth dwellers. God has raised those who have brought His prophetic warnings in more recent decades. But a very low percentage of those who hear have really listened. The saddest part is that God's own people are not listening. In many cases, they are not even being told by their own pastors and teachers the message that Christ could return at any moment. Christians are not being informed that there are no signs that must precede His sudden coming in the air for His saints!

Too many pastors preach a message of "feel-goodism" and "do-goodism." Theirs is a social gospel meant to make the people in the pews comfortable. The deeper the people are into their comfort zones, the better it makes these preachers feel.

Satan sees no reason to disrupt such tranquility in a church. With pastors and their flocks under feel-goodism and do-goodism sedation, he can devote more time to planning exactly how to turn the planet into hell on Earth.

Time To Plug In!

God's power is available. It is a high-voltage energizer that can infuse the Christian with strength for these closing days we face. The study of Bible prophecy excites the students who earnestly desire to learn what God wants them to know. A person's worldview, when a child of God looks into the future through God's omniscient eyes, separates from the gloomy worldview of those who see life on Earth coming to an end because of global warming, an asteroid impact, or thermonuclear war. These things, according to some descriptions found in Revelation and other prophetic books of the Bible, might lurk in the future. But Christians who truly understand what God wants them to know about things to come have no dread of that future, whatever it might hold.

The student who is attuned to the prophetic Word also is given wisdom to understand that all humanistic efforts to create utopia on earth will fail, just as they always have. Only under the Reign of King Jesus will people truly prosper.

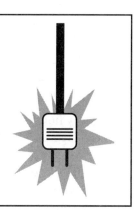

PLUG IN TO GOD'S POWER FOR:

- strength to face the future
- a growing desire to learn God's Word
- a changed—more godly—world-view
- wisdom
- excitement, not dread, about the time to come

World Without End

It is certain, according to God's prophetic Word, that people are in for some terrible times. But, the world will never end. Christians can look forward to a thrilling moment in time when we suddenly find ourselves in the marvelous presence of our Lord and Savior, Jesus Christ. This is true whether we die, or whether we are raptured in a moment, in the twinkling of an eye!

When Christians die they are instantly in the presence of Christ. Paul the Apostle said: "We are confident, I say, and willing rather to be absent from the body, and to be present with the Lord" (2 Cor. 5:8). Paul says further: "For whether we live, we live unto the Lord; and whether we die, we die unto the Lord: whether we live therefore, or die, we are the Lord's" (Rom. 14:8).

One Thrilling Moment

When the rapture of the saints occurs, Christians will be with their Lord instantly and for eternity. Again, the Apostle Paul tells what will happen to the bodies of the dead and of those who are alive when this stunning event takes place: "Then we which are alive and remain shall be caught up together with them in the clouds, to meet the Lord in the air: and so shall we ever be with the Lord" (1 Thess. 4:17). We will look closely at all associated with this thrilling prophetic event in a future part of this study. But, for now, let's look at what we should be doing in anticipation of its any-moment occurrence.

The Prophecy-Powered Christian

Exactly how should the Christian conduct his life in view of coming face to face with Jesus—whether through death, or through rapture? The Apostle Peter had something profound to say about the matter: "Seeing then that all these things shall be dissolved, what manner of persons ought ye to be in all holy conversation and godliness, Looking for and hasting unto the coming of the day of God, wherein the heavens being on fire shall be dissolved, and the elements shall melt with fervent heat? Nevertheless we, according to his promise, look for new heavens and a new earth, wherein dwelleth righteousness. Wherefore, beloved, seeing that ye look for such things, be diligent that ye may be found of him in peace, without spot, and blameless" (2 Peter 3:11-14).

The Day of the Lord

Peter, the great apostle and earliest disciple of Jesus, tells Christians that they should first look for the coming of the "day of the Lord." The "day of the Lord" will begin with that terrible time—that seven-year era of tribulation also known as "Daniel's seventieth week" and "the time of Jacob's trouble." It will be the worst time in human history, according to Jesus and Jeremiah the prophet. Why should Christians be looking for such a horrendous time?

That time will see a series of three terrible manifestations of God's righteous wrath, each of the three including seven judgments, for a total of 21 specific judgments. Each judgment that falls upon incorrigibly wicked, rebellious Earth-dwellers of that time will grow progressively more punishing. Things will get so bad that people will try to hide themselves in the caves and crevices of mountains to get away from God's

Wrath. They will come to the point they will beg the mountains to fall on them.

Why Look for Trouble?

Why would Peter tell Christians to look for these things to hurry and come? Actually, the apostle Peter is telling us to consider these things in the most serious terms and to heed God's prophetic words on that coming era of horror. The key part of this prophetic passage God wants us to understand is: "Seeing then that all these things shall be dissolved, what manner of persons ought ye to be in all holy conversation and godliness?" Christians are to think upon these coming judgments, and in thinking upon them with all prayerful seriousness, our lives will be changed into lives of godliness.

Concern for the Doomed

We, as God's children, can understand—if we apply ourselves to knowing prophecy—the things people of the tribulation will have to endure because of their rebellion, or their sin. We are expected, as Christians, to know, through Bible prophecy, these things to come.

We aren't expected to know about those coming judgments because God wants us to fear going through them ourselves. We are to understand them out of love for those who, if they do not repent and come to a saving knowledge of Christ, this side of the rapture, will have to go through that time of horrors.

Not Destined for God's Wrath

Knowledge of Bible prophecy—of future events—will make us more holy and godly in our conduct of our own lives. It will make us more dedicated witnesses for the cause of Christ. Christians are not appointed to God's wrath, according to 1 Thessalonians 5:9. We are to comfort each other with that knowledge according to 1 Thessalonians 5:11. Our future is secure in Jesus. Our concern should be for others who don't know Him in an intimate, saving way. We are also to be looking for that "day of the Lord" because before it starts, Jesus will come for us and say, "Come up hither" (Rev. 4:1).

Jesus Is No Thief

Jesus Himself compared His coming to the coming of a "thief in the night." Why would the sinless Creator-God of all the universes compare Himself to a thief in the night? Jesus' return to Earth will be in two phases. First will come the Rapture, then, at least seven years later, His glorious appearance. This description of the first phase of Christ's Second Coming is found in Peter's prophecy: "But the day of the Lord will come as a thief in the night; in the which the heavens shall pass away with a great noise, and the elements shall melt with fervent heat, the earth also and the works that are therein shall be burned up" (2 Peter 3:10).

A thief comes unannounced. He breaks into a tranquil setting, such as one's home, and takes something. Jesus was forewarning that He will intervene in the affairs of mankind with a sudden, silent taking away of something. That "something" is His saints—all who were saved.

From Rapture to Re-creation of Earth

The entire "day of the Lord" then will run its course until the end of Christ's millennial reign, the Great White Throne Judgment and the remaking of the heavens and the earth.

His coming "as a thief in the night" can't be the Second Coming or Second Advent of Christ to set up His rule and reign in Jerusalem at the end of the great war called Armageddon. Every eye will see Him returning at that time.

The King Cometh!

The prophetic Word foretells the second phase of Christ's Second Coming—His return to planet Earth in power and glory, as follows: "And I saw heaven opened, and behold a white horse; and he that sat upon him was called Faithful and True, and in righteousness he doth judge and make war. His eyes were as a flame of fire, and on his head were many crowns; and he had a name written, that no man knew, but he himself. And he was clothed with a vesture dipped in blood: and his name is called The Word of God. And the armies which were in heaven followed him upon white horses, clothed in fine linen, white and clean. And out of his mouth goeth a sharp sword, that with it he should smite the nations: and he shall rule them with a rod of iron: and he treadeth the winepress of the fierceness and wrath of Almighty God. And he hath on his vesture and on his thigh a name written, KING OF KINGS, AND LORD OF LORDS" (Rev. 19:11-16).

Be assured: absolutely no one will miss that glorious appearance!

Jesus Keeps His Promises

At least seven years before that return in the clouds of glory, the Rapture will occur. Jesus, in His "thief in the night" coming, will fulfill His own words: "Let not your heart be troubled: ye believe in God, believe also in me. In my Father's house are many mansions: if it were not so, I would have told you. I go to prepare a place for you. And if I go and prepare a place for you, I will come again, and receive you unto myself; that where I am, there ye may be also" (John 14:1-3).

We Christians are to be looking toward the "day of the Lord" and desiring its soon coming, because Jesus, before that day begins, will come to take us home to Heaven with Him to live eternally in magnificent dwelling places He has prepared for us.

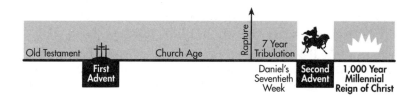

Christians Must Watch

About looking for His coming for His saints in the Rapture, the Lord instructed all whom would be saved, "And what I say unto you I say unto all, Watch" (Mark 13:37). Until that exhilarating moment of Rapture, Christians are to be power-filled sentries! What, exactly, does this duty entail?

The Power-Filled Sentry

No other generation in history has been privileged to see end-time things developing as has the present generation. Notice the word *developing*. These last-days signals are not prophecy being fulfilled. The signals consist of issues and events that are setting the stage for fulfillment of Bible prophecy.

It is proper to liken these stage-setting issues and events to a dark, ominous storm that is boiling on the distant horizon. We can see the apocalyptic tempest coming, with jagged flashes of lightning fracturing the black, rolling clouds. But we aren't yet in the storm. We know it's approaching with great swiftness, and it is our job to warn others before it's too late!

Watch God's Radar Screen

Just as a person couldn't issue an accurate tornado warning if he couldn't read the radar signals on the monitors of his weather computers, the Christian can't warn of prophetic things to come without knowledge of the signals provided in God's Word.

We must become good students by studying prophecy, as well as the other parts of the Bible. We are instructed: "Study to shew thyself approved unto God, a workman that needeth not to be ashamed, rightly dividing the word of truth" (2 Tim. 2:15). Note that the Apostle Paul didn't tell us—under inspiration of the Holy Spirit—to study "part" of God's Word. He said to "study . . . rightly dividing the word of truth." That's a direct order to study the whole Bible, not just parts. This is where God's people are failing today. We are to not only study the whole Word of God, but we are also to study our times to determine where we stand on God's prophetic timeline. Jesus scolded the Pharisees also with the Sadducees who, as they always did, sought to trick Him into giving false prophecy so they could accuse Him, legally. He answered them as follows: "When it is evening, ye say, It will be fair weather: for the sky is red. And in the morning, It will be foul weather to day: for the sky is red and lowring. O ye hypocrites, ye can discern the face of the sky; but can ye not discern the signs of the times?" (Matt. 16:2, 3). If these pious, pompous, self-proclaimed holy men had known the signals around them, they would have realized that it was the time of Israel's visitation by the Messiah Himself! They should have been able to discern the signs of their times, but they could not.

Many signals today indicate that the Messiah is about to visit planet Earth once again. This time as King of kings and Lord of lords! We as Christians must be good sentries, filled with God-given power of prophetic discernment. The only way to serve in this duty is to study the prophetic word and pray for understanding. We must then look at the signals in that Holy Spirit-given ability to comprehend our times.

Some Signals To Watch

We will go into them in deeper details elsewhere in this study, but a few things for the power-filled sentry to look for, along with undertaking intensive study and prayer, are the following:

- **The characteristics of end-time mankind.** Some of these have already been mentioned. A good representation of what mankind will be like at the end of the age, just before Christ's return, is found in 2 Timothy 3:1-9.
- **The development of the last kingdom described in Daniel's dream-vision.** Daniel interpreted Nebuchadnezzar's dream, as told in Daniel, chapter 2. Then Daniel had a night-vision himself as told in Daniel, chapter 7. He saw a fifth beast that was strong and terrible. Many observers of prophecy believe we see the coming of that final form of world government in our day.
- **The events taking place in and concerning Israel.** Israel is the most profound signal of all of where we stand on God's prophetic timeline. The nation of Israel was born (reborn, actually) on a single day, just as prophesied. It is back in the land to fulfill its prophetic destiny as the head of nations. First, however, Israel will have to endure the most horrific period of persecution there has ever been in human history. We must watch the nation of Israel carefully in our hourly news. We can learn much about how near we are to Christ's return by doing so.

The power-filled sentry is one who works to sow the seeds of the gospel while he goes through daily life. The sentry, at the same time, continually observes things around him and realizes that the coming of Jesus Christ cannot be far off. That coming will be one in which millions will vanish from earth in a moment, in the twinkling of an eye!

We are instructed: "And when these things begin to come to pass, then look up, and lift up your heads; for your redemption draweth nigh" (Luke 21:28).

For Additional Study

1. What did Jesus say about the time He will come back in the Rapture?

2. What other times in history did Jesus compare to His coming again?

3. What were those times like, just before catastrophes fell?

4. What sign must there be before the Rapture?

5. What can the study of Bible prophecy do for the believer?

6. As students of Bible prophecy, how should we be conducting ourselves?

7. What is the Day of the Lord?

8. How many specific judgments from God are there prophetically scheduled for the Tribulation?

9. Why should Christians understand these horrible things to come?

10. Give the best passage to point out that Christians of the Church Age aren't to endure God's Wrath in the Tribulation.

11. List the two phases of Christ's Second Coming.

Scoffers and Scoundrels

KEY PROPHECY POWER TRUTH

"Knowing this first, that there shall come in the last days scoffers, walking after their own lusts, and saying, Where is the promise of his coming?"

2 Peter 3: 3, 4

Two prophetic passages speak to our generation as perhaps no others. God inspired the apostles, Peter and Paul, to forewarn of a chief characteristic that will mark the generation alive at the time Jesus returns for His saints at the Rapture. The Apostle Paul writes: "This know also, that in the last days perilous times shall come [for people will come on the scene]. Having a form of godliness, but denying the power thereof: from such turn away. For of this sort are they which creep into houses, and lead captive silly women laden with sins, led away with divers lusts, Ever learning, and never able to come to the knowledge of the truth" (2 Tim. 3:1, 5-7).

While Paul's words are more general in describing anti-God characteristics that will mark the end of the Age, Peter focuses in precisely on one particular manifestation Paul's prophecy is addressing. "Knowing this first, that there shall come in the last days scoffers, walking after their own lusts, And saying, Where is the promise of his coming? for since the fathers fell asleep, all things continue as they were from the beginning of the creation. For this they willingly are ignorant of, that by the word of God the heavens were of old, and the earth standing out of the water and in the water: Whereby the world that then was, being overflowed with water, perished: But the heavens and the earth, which are now, by the same word are kept in store, reserved unto fire against the day of judgment and perdition of ungodly men" (2 Peter 3:3-7).

Scoffers Abound

• Scoffers of Science

The world's scientific community dogmatically adheres to a doctrine more faith-based than is the belief that God created the heavens and earth. They refuse to allow any other system to be taught in public schools than that which puts forth that all life on earth evolved to what we see around us now. From some mysterious spark somewhere in the nothingness of the past, a "big bang" occurred, and things started happening— although they can't quite get a handle on exactly what started to happen. A primordial slime of some sort developed from this burst of nothingness, and from that eventually emerged life. And, here we stand today—man!

Of course, this took billions and billions of years, as a famous now deceased scientist used to say. The "animal" called man evolved through a series of evolutionary leaps from one specie to another, the gods of science tell us, until the final leap from the monkey form of primate to the *homo sapien* form. Then man went through various versions up to Neanderthal, then made the final leap to the brilliant creatures scientists claim to now be.

The Real Kooks?

Only problem: they can't find even one missing link at any point along their evolutionary chain—despite claiming that a deformed skeleton they call "Lucy" was such a transition form. (Remember, these are the same folks who invented a complete profile on what they called a pre-modern man called "Piltdown Man" from a single tooth!) And they call us, who believe in the creation by Almighty God, kooks! One former network news anchor who some once called "the most trusted man in America," did a lengthy series all about our "ancestor," "Neanderthal Man." Now, however, scientists are backtracking on the many "scientific findings" of propaganda such as that presented in the well-known series.

A Change of Tune

Here's what the scientists have learned as of late:

"Reuters

Tue Jan 27, [2004] 6:09 AM ET By Maggie Fox, Health and Science Correspondent

WASHINGTON (Reuters) - You may think your grandparents act like Neanderthals, but U.S. researchers said on Monday they had strong evidence that modern humans are not descended from them ...

... New York University paleoanthropologist Katerina Harvati said Neanderthals should be considered a separate species from Homo sapiens, and not just a sub-species ...

Yet, even faced with the stark evidence that there's no connection, this scientist still holds that these creatures could still be some form of human—type beings, the story went on to indicate. Scientists, for the most part, scoff at a God that intervenes in the affairs of mankind.

• Scoffers in the Sanctuaries

Scoffing from science is sad, even tragic. But, the scoffing that goes on in the sanctuaries and among others who claim to be children of God through Christ is blasphemous.

Satan is at the heart of such unbelief; make no mistake!

Liberal-minded theologians who believe that God's Word, the Bible, isn't divinely inspired, are not the most terrible thing about the scoffing. These can't discern truth, because they don't know the Truth-Giver. Preachers and teachers who truly believe that Christ's atoning blood alone saves the sinner, yet believe, and proclaim that there are no prophecies yet to be fulfilled is where the most horrendous error resides. That's the really tragic part in the matter of scoffing at the notion that Jesus will come back like He promised.

Spirit of Antichrist

This brings us to another strong indicator that this generation is bumping up against the end of the age. The Apostle John wrote: "Beloved, believe not every spirit, but try the spirits whether they are of God: because many false prophets are gone out into the world. Hereby know ye the Spirit of God: Every spirit that confesseth that Jesus Christ is come in the flesh is of God: And every spirit that confesseth not that Jesus Christ is come in the flesh is not of God: and this is that spirit of antichrist, whereof ye have heard that it should come; and even now already is it in the world" (1 John 4:1-3).

Jesus Is Jewish!

Jesus was born to a Jewish mother. He was, is, and will return as the Jewish Messiah, and the King of the Jews. Jesus is also King of all kings and Lord of all lords, but His Jewishness must not be diminished! To do so is to join in with the worldview wherein resides the "spirit of Antichrist." That evil spirit, John says under inspiration, declares that Jesus was not a Jew, and will not return to reign and rule as the King of the Jews upon the Jewish King David's throne as God's prophecy plainly foretells.

Heart of the Problem

Those theologians who don't believe God's Word about the salvation process required by a holy, righteous God can't be expected to see Jesus as having a special relationship with Jews and the nation of Israel. As stated above, they can't know truth, because they would rather believe Satan's lies.

However, pastors, teachers, and others who believe that Christ died for the sin of mankind, yet deny that God will also save Israel (the one-third remnant of Jews who make it through the Tribulation), are willingly ignorant. They willfully accept, even adamantly proclaim, that churches now are the inheritor of all the promises God made to Israel. This "replacement theology" is a big part of the heresy tied up in the termed "spirit of Antichrist."

They are telling God that His Word is only partly true. They are telling Jesus that He will not rule and reign on the throne of David from Jerusalem. This is no different than what the apostate religionists and the secular humanists say about the Bible, and about the nation of Israel.

The Godly View

But the Lord has a far different perspective. He said to Abraham, the patriarch of all Israel: "And I will make of thee a great nation, and I will bless thee, and make thy name great; and thou shalt be a blessing: And I will bless them that bless thee, and curse him that curseth thee: and in thee shall all families of the earth be blessed" (Gen. 12:2, 3).

About God's promise to Israel, Moses said to all the people of that nation: "For thou art an holy people unto the LORD thy God: the LORD thy God hath chosen thee to be a special people unto himself, above all people that are upon the face of the earth" (Deut. 7:6).

King David confirmed God's commitment to the nation when he said: "For thou hast confirmed to thyself thy people Israel to be a people unto thee for ever: and thou, LORD, art become their God" (2 Sam. 7:24).

God declared that His promises to Israel, in regard to His blessings of nationhood, will never fail. Israel will possess all things their God promised them—including the vast land He promised—forever!

Antichrist Spirit Alive and Well on Planet Earth

The "spirit of Antichrist" is alive, and working against the cause of Christ, which is the desire that all come to Him for salvation. The self-centered scoffing by those who declare they are doing God's work, yet who deny that God's Son, a Jew, will rule over Israel and the world from the Jewish throne of David adds to the Antichrist spirit's ammunition. It's time for Christians to wake up!

Scoundrels, like Predators

Remember the Apostle Paul's words: "This know also, that in the last days perilous times shall come [for people will come on the scene]. Having a form of godliness, but denying the power thereof: from such turn away. For of this sort are they which creep into houses, and lead captive silly women laden with sins, led away with divers lusts, Ever learning, and never able to come to the knowledge of the truth" (2 Tim. 3:1, 5-7).

The great apostle prophesied that the last days will be marked by the appearance of those who will look as if they were godly, but won't really care about the true power of God's dealing with mankind. They push the buttons of greed. They proclaim the power of prosperity, here and now.

The All-Powerful Jesus

The real power God wants to give men and women, boys and girls, is the power found in Jesus Christ. Paul also wrote of that awesome power, and his fervent desire to know Christ in His fullness: "That I may know him, and the power of his resurrection, and the fellowship of his sufferings, being made conformable unto his death" (Phil. 3:10).

The true power is in Jesus to give eternal life to anyone who will accept that grace gift from Christ's heavenly Father. Eternal life begins with the new birth (being born again) and will leap into its fullness at the believer's death, or at the Rapture. About this, John wrote further: "Beloved, now are we the sons of God, and it doth not yet appear what we shall be: but we know that, when he shall appear, we shall be like him; for we shall see him as he is" (1 John 3:2).

Strength Through Love

When we have the power of Jesus, we are strong through His strength. Our desire is to share Him, and His whole Word, with others. This is the love Jesus was talking about when He said: "And thou shalt love the Lord thy God with all thy heart, and with all thy soul, and with all thy mind, and with all thy strength: this is the first commandment. And the second is like, namely this, Thou shalt love thy neighbour as thyself. There is none other commandment greater than these" (Mark 12:30, 31).

Scoundrels' Seductive Sales Pitch

Paul says that those who appear to have a form of godliness but deny the true power of Christ will sneak into houses and lead their gullible victims captive with their words. The ungodly seducers will make merchandise of people who are always trying to learn a new, different message, other than the true lessons given through the Word of God.

Peter expands upon those false teachers and the ones upon whom they prey in the following Scripture: "And through covetousness shall they with feigned words make merchandise of you: whose judgment now of a long time lingereth not, and their damnation slumbereth not" (2 Peter 2:3).

Wolves Among Us

The wolves in sheep's clothing who come in and delude the gullible are covetous of money. One doesn't have to punch the remote too many times while clicking through the TV channels today to soon find one or the other of these "covetous" people with a godly tone, but an ungodly message, making merchandise of the willingly ignorant flock.

Power of Prophecy

Scoundrels are among us. It is one more signal that we are near the time Jesus will call His own to be with Him in the Rapture. God doesn't want His children to be taken off guard—or taken in. He wants us to be vigilant—to see the wolves in the sheep's clothing for what they are.

That's what His prophetic Word is all about. It is to forewarn of things to come. The diligent student of the whole Word of God can't be fooled by those who are interested only in fleecing him. The informed, discerning student of Bible prophecy will understand that the false teachers' messages are on the airwaves so the predators can live in compounds of several mansion-type homes, drive luxury vehicles, wear extravagant clothing and ultra-expensive jewelry.

The false view of God-promised prosperity can't deceive the spiritually attuned mind that is forewarned by prophecy from the Bible.

Seek Empowerment from on High

We must seek to be empowered children of God—empowered to resist the deception foretold for the closing days of human history. Jesus forewarned: "For there shall arise false Christs, and false prophets, and shall shew great signs and wonders; insomuch that, if it were possible, they shall deceive the very elect" (Matt. 24:24).

This prophecy was given for the Great Tribulation, that last three and one-half years of the seven years of God's wrath. Before that era of apocalypse, Christ will call His saints home. So, it will not be possible for God's children of the Church Age to be deceived by the false teachers of that Tribulation Period.

Those who come to know Christ during that time will, of course, be supernaturally protected from the delusion.

Almost in the Storm!

However, we learned before that we can see the Tribulation storm front approaching in our troubled day. The tempest contains many signals of the prophesied full-blown hurricane of apocalypse.

Just as hurricanes send out tropical fronts or impulses in advance of the great storms themselves, so the Tribulation storm is sending out impulses that include false teaching and false prophecy. In that sense, Jesus' forewarning applies to Christians today. We must be on our guard. Understanding true Bible prophecy gives us the power to protect against such fiery darts from Satan and his minions.

Facing Up to Evil

Let's again look at the Scriptures forewarning of "the spirit of Antichrist," and how we must face up to such evil. John the apostle prophesied: "Beloved, believe not every spirit, but try the spirits whether they are of God: because many false prophets are gone out into the world. Hereby know ye the Spirit of God: Every spirit that confesseth that Jesus Christ is come in the flesh is of God: And every spirit that confesseth not that Jesus Christ is come in the flesh is not of God: and this is that spirit of antichrist, whereof ye have heard that it should come; and even now already is it in the world. Ye are of God, little children, and have overcome them: because greater is he that is in you, than he that is in the world. They are of the world: therefore speak they of the world, and the world heareth them. We are of God: he that knoweth God heareth us; he that is not of God heareth not us. Hereby know we the spirit of truth, and the spirit of error" (1 John 4:1-6).

Prophecy Protects Against Pretenders

A good understanding of Bible prophecy can prevent us from falling victim to the pretenders Satan wants to use to lure us in to false views—and worse. John tells us in this 1 John 4:1-6 prophetic forewarning so relevant to our time:

- We are to be extremely wary of every strange thing we hear regarding teachings supposedly from the Bible.
- We must search the Scriptures and pray for discernment from the Holy Spirit to make sure the teachings we hear are given by God.
- John warns that even in his time, Satan had sent many false prophets and teachers were doing their soul-destroying work
- First thing to know is that the teacher must confess that Jesus Christ, alone, has come into the world—in the flesh, as the God-man—to seek and save the lost.
- Every teacher or theological position that denies the virgin birth, death, burial and resurrection of Christ is of the devil, not of God.
- If we are God's true children, we have already overcome all of the pretenders and their lies, through Christ. That's tremendous power!
- Beware of all who understand only things of the world, and not the things of God. These must be given the gospel of Christ, not joined in their worldly lusts.
- We can know that if others understand and agree with us on who Jesus truly is, then they belong to the Father. Any other view is from a spirit of error, and we must resist that spirit.

Power-Filled, Prophetic Prayer

Jesus prayed a mighty prayer that included each of us who claim His name today. His prayer was prophetic, and filled with His great power to influence the lives of His "sheep" down through the ages. The Lord prayed to His Father: "And now come I to thee; and these things I speak in the world, that they might have my joy fulfilled in themselves. I have given them thy word; and the world hath hated them, because they are not of the world, even as I am not of the world. I pray not that thou shouldest take them out of the world, but that thou shouldest keep them from the evil. They are not of the world, even as I am not of the world. Sanctify them through thy truth: thy word is truth. As thou hast sent me into the world, even so have I also sent them into the world. And for their sakes I sanctify myself, that they also might be sanctified through the truth. Neither pray I for these alone, but for them also which shall believe on me through their word; That they all may be one; as thou, Father, art in me, and I in thee, that they also may be one in us: that the world may believe that thou hast sent me. And the glory which thou gavest me I have given them; that they may be one, even as we are one: I in them, and thou in me, that they may be made perfect in one; and that the world may know that thou hast sent me, and hast loved them, as thou hast loved me. Father, I will that they also, whom thou hast given me, be with me where I am; that they may behold my glory, which thou hast given me: for thou lovedst me before the foundation of the world. O righteous Father, the world hath not known thee: but I have known thee, and these have known that thou hast sent me. And I have declared unto them thy name, and will declare it: that the love wherewith thou hast loved me may be in them, and I in them" (John 17:13-26).

What a powerful, prophetic prayer for you and me! What a mighty Lord we serve!

For Additional Study

1. What is the Scripture passage that best demonstrates the last-days scoffing at Christ's coming again?

2. What is the number 1 scientific problem with the theory of evolution?

3. What is the ultimate source of scoffing about Creation by God, and the return of Christ?

4. What is the evil spirit called which mocks Jesus' first and second comings?

5. Has the church replaced Israel in God's promises for that nation?

6. Give a Scriptural reference from Israel's King David that proves God's promises to that nation are forever.

7. What is the power of godly love, and what desire does it produce?

8. What does the Bible mean that some will desire to make merchandise of the saints?

9. What can prophecy do to help with this end-time problem?

Overpowering These Perilous Times

KEY PROPHECY POWER TRUTH

"Ye are of God, little children, and have overcome them: because greater is he that is in you, than he that is in the world."

1 John 4:4

There was a time, early in the 20th century, when reports of children being sold to makers of pornographic movies and magazines would have been met with disbelief by the reader or hearer of such allegations. The Internet, of course, wasn't yet even on the horizon of our culture.

Explosion of Evil

News of gang violence, mass killings, of genocide on an unfathomable scale would have—among civilized people at least—been considered as acts of barbarism predating the Renaissance or as happening only in earth's most primitive cultures. Almost certainly, such acts in early twentieth century life would have been cataloged as aberrations or isolated incidents of insanity. The century just past ended with society and culture in the U.S. exploding with every conceivable debased human activity. The symptoms of end-time man were everywhere—all the time.

Symptoms of the "perilous times" the Apostle Paul prophesied for the last days continue to pop up in every direction we look.

Politicians Have "I" Trouble

Among the most prominent of these signals that we might be at the very end of the age, just before Jesus calls His saints to be with Him, are the ones the great apostle termed "covetous, boasters, proud." It isn't the purpose of this study, or of this writer, to become involved in the political process of presidential politics. The study doesn't intentionally put forward either of the major or any of the marginal parties on the American political scene.

However, in flipping through some of the early morning shows on cable and network television, the presidential hopefuls in recent presidential primaries dominated the airwaves. No matter who was being interviewed, the rhetoric was the same:

- "I can do this better than the president."
- "I'm the only candidate who can bring peace.
- "The others offer nothing of substance; I, on the other hand, have always been able to . . . "
- "I am the only one with military experience, plus administrative expertise."
- "I'm the only logical candidate for president."

It's "me, me, I, I" on every channel where these folks appear. Now, we all know that this is the political process in America. We've created it. Studies show that a candidate who doesn't do these self-promotions is more often than not perceived as weak, unsure, like a wildebeest out on the African plains that is too weak and sickly to keep up with the herd. The lions and hyenas can pick it off without much effort.

Paul said that men will be lovers of themselves, covetous, boasters, proud. Certainly each of the candidates within the American political process comes across as exhibiting these characteristics. It seems that more than ever, during presidential season, the rhetoric and self-aggrandizement are consistently on an elevated, or maybe that should be a debased, scale.

No matter the particular election, the candidates seem to throw snowballs at others in the race that have rocks at their centers. They seem meant to bloody, not just make the others look all wet in their views.

No matter the party, we can be certain that when the other party gets officially more involved in the political fray, the rock-filled snowballs—or mudballs—will be flying from both sides with equal hatred behind them. This evokes thoughts of another of the end-time symptoms Paul mentioned: "Men shall be . . . fierce."

An Addictive Generation

Paul prophesied that the last-days generation will be filled with people who are "incontinent." This word doesn't, in this case, mean they need adult diapers. The word means "addicted to an uncontrolled degree," that is, people of the last-days earth scene will be easily addicted to various things, and will be out of control with their addictions.

Considering the obvious, it's easy to understand that this is an addictive generation. Drugs, both illicit and prescription, are in demand. Most of the drugs are initially taken because they make the person using them feel better through relieving pain, whether physical, or psychological. The person who becomes addicted then must have them, or the pain returns with greater intensity. Then, they must increase dosage to just stay ahead of the growing cravings they suffer. It is a never-ending spiral into decline in sanity and health, if not dealt with through appropriate measures.

Many Addictions

Statistics demonstrate that this type of addiction is becoming pandemic. But, drugs are only one class of addictions in these closing days of this age. People become addicted to many things. Television viewing is one such addiction. Sexual addiction is another. Internet pornography is perhaps the most frightening of this entire category of addictiveness.

People become addicted to sports, to making money, to spending money, to gambling and to many other things.

Violating God's Commandment

In effect, this "incontinence," this addictive behavior, is violating the greatest principle put forward by the Lord Jesus.

We can best understand by heeding His words in the following passage:

"And one of the scribes came, and having heard them reasoning together, and perceiving that he had answered them well, asked him, Which is the first commandment of all? And Jesus answered him, The first of all the commandments is, Hear, O Israel; The Lord our God is one Lord: And thou shalt love the Lord thy God with all thy heart, and with all thy soul, and with all thy mind, and with all thy strength: this is the first commandment" (Mark 12:28-30).

Anyone or anything we put before the Lord is an idol. Idolatrous worship is akin to addiction, in that we put things number one in our lives, above our love for God. Jesus said in Matthew 6:24: "No man can serve two masters: for either he will hate the one, and love the other; or else he will hold to the one, and despise the other."

Other Gods

We worship celebrity, money, homes, clothes, our children, self-improvement, dieting, and a hundred other things, when we put them above God. I didn't say this, God said it through His Word, the Lord Jesus Christ. I write to myself, as well as to you. We must begin, as Christians, to put God first in all things. It is the greatest of all God's commandments. We were created by Him, and for Him. We are to worship Him, and Him alone.

Perhaps the most condemning of all of the prophecies Paul gave in his 2 Timothy, chapter 3 account of last-days symptoms is: "Men shall be . . . lovers of pleasures more than lovers of God" (verses 2, 4).

On the Brink

It isn't hard to discern that we stand at the extremity of the Church Age when we seriously consider the apostle's forewarnings of the characteristics of last-days mankind. This is all the more reason we should be watching, in anticipation of Christ's call: "Come up hither!" (Rev. 4:1).

Although we've looked at a few of the sinister characteristics so prevalent in this "last time," as John the Apostle called it in 1 John 2:18, we will examine our culture and society a bit closer.

Worse and Worse

In 2 Timothy 3:13 the Apostle Paul, under inspiration of the Holy Spirit, prophesied: "But evil men and seducers shall wax worse and worse." From the daily news accounts, the accuracy of this prophecy cannot be denied. The front pages of our newspapers do not provide adequate space to contain the number of stories flowing from the news services across America and the world. TV news is overwhelmed, so that the latest news shocker is quickly replaced by the next. Even the seemingly limitless cyberspace of Internet is challenged to capture all the bad news!

Reports of man's degenerate acts spill over into and fill other pages from front to back, no matter the medium. The rare exception in today's world is the story of people doing something beneficial to help others; the norm is bad news.

End-Time Flood Predicted

The Scriptures tell us that the end will come like a flood. All the signs given by God's prophetic Word will be gushing through the generation that is alive at the time Jesus Christ returns to put an end to man's insanity. While the Apocalypse looms and Armageddon sucks all of fallen mankind into its vortex, the time will resemble the days of Noah and the days of Lot.

Jesus said in Luke 21:28: "And when these things begin to come to pass, then look up, and lift up your heads; for your redemption draweth nigh."

Unlike Any Other Generation

Jesus was speaking to His disciples of every generation, but particularly to His disciples, or followers, who would be alive at the end of the age. There has never been a generation in which all signs prophesied for the last days have come as a flood until this generation. In this passage the Lord was telling His saints who would be living during the end-time period to be watchful and expectant. He promised He would come for them when the signs given in prophecy begin to manifest themselves. Let us consider how near that time must be.

Major End-Time Characteristics

The major symptoms of fallen humanity's end-time societal disorder are given by Paul's prophecy in 2 Timothy. We will look briefly at a few recent current issues and dissect these matters one at a time, filtering them through the light of God's prophetic Word.

Again, we must look at the forewarnings given by Paul. "This know also, that in the last days perilous times shall come. For men shall be lovers of their own selves, covetous, boasters, proud, blasphemers, disobedient to parents, unthankful, unholy, without natural affection, trucebreakers, false accusers, incontinent, fierce, despisers of those that are good, traitors, heady, highminded, lovers of pleasures more than lovers of God; Having a form of godliness, but denying the power thereof: from such turn away" (2 Tim. 3:1-5).

Symptom #1: Lovers of Self

Poor us. Today we are told by sociologists and by psychologists that, at the root of practically every personality problem, is lack of self-esteem. Criminals, deprived of equality in society as children, thus grow up feeling left at the bottom of the heap and become angry at the system that rejected them. They rationalize that it is street justice to compensate for what society has done to hurt them, and, therefore, society is fair game.

Psychologists say people should be taught to acquire higher self-esteem; then they will become useful, productive citizens. Self-esteem is another expression for self-love, and God's Word says that this inward-turned philosophy is the problem—not the cure. When people think first and foremost of themselves, others whose lives they affect inevitably suffer from their self-indulgence. We can plainly see the sociologists are wrong. The crime rates are on the rise!

Symptom #2: Coveters

Keeping up with the Joneses is more than a joke in America today; it is symptomatic of a society gone mad with compulsion to acquire not merely as much as one's neighbor, but much more than one's neighbor. Commercials have for years told us that we "deserve the best" and have urged us to "go for the gusto." We continue to have our senses assaulted by advertising slogans that appeal to our human pride—to our love of self.

This materialistic drive has individually, nationally and globally tumbled man into an economic abyss from which he will not be extricated, apart from the unprecedented (and ultimately diabolical) geopolitical and socioeconomic rearrangement prophesied in Revelation 13. Rock star Madonna's hit song from some years ago, "Material Girl," says precisely what this generation is becoming.

Symptoms #3, #4: Boasters, Proud

Following closely on the heels of covetousness—actually an outgrowth of it—are the dual vanities within the heart of end-time man. These people are boasters; they are extremely proud.

Jesus said, "Blessed are the meek [humble]: for they shall inherit the earth [the millennial earth]" (Matt. 5:5).

The father of those whose characters exhibit the antithesis of humility is Satan. Lucifer was the greatest boaster of them all. "I will exalt my throne above the stars of God" (Isa. 14:13), he said in his supremely prideful arrogance. He seduced Eve in the Garden of Eden with the same prideful boast and promise. "Ye shall be as gods," he told her. When Adam yielded, all humankind became a genetic heir to the great pride that first welled in Lucifer's heart.

Again, we see the boasting and the pride in our children. We can remember our own childhood experiences. We made claims, each having to be bigger and better or farther or faster than the boast that went before.

Again, we know that politicians are living, breathing proof of boastfulness and pride, while they vie for a chance to "serve" us. How quickly the boasts turn bitter and ring hollow when they become inaccessible and self-willed after election time. They become little lords; we become revenue producers for the wastefulness of bureaucracy. The rhetoric of the campaign stump, whether on the courthouse lawn, door to door, or in media propaganda is a strange alchemy of prideful boasting and humble exhortation.

Yet we who are victimized time after time have no room to complain; it is the American political process in action. It is the process we have allowed to stray far from the noble designs of the founding fathers, a process we perpetuate through our acquiescence. This is not cynicism—it is fact.

Symptom #5: Blasphemy

God's name has been all but officially removed from public education in America—in itself a blasphemous thing. But His name is at the same time in practically every theater in America. Jesus Christ is unmentionable in public forums because His Holy Name represents a narrow-minded viewpoint and would offend. Religion, if it is to be mentioned, must represent an eclectic view—must encompass an ecumenical theological viewpoint.

In almost every film above the rating of "G," the name of Jesus Christ is repeated frequently. It seems, as a matter of fact, as if screenwriters are required to use His Holy Name blasphemously at least a minimum number of times per scene. Always, the name of God, the name of Jesus, is used in one of two ways: 1) as an expression of frustration, exasperation, or anger; or 2) to portray the fanaticism of one religious zealot or another, usually a character who is dangerously insane.

Is it any wonder that a blasphemous generation of young people reject discipline and self-control, when adults have spent decades producing an anti-God language? Even Christian parents have slowly become desensitized, thereby giving into this blasphemous language's insidious, venomous effects.

Symptom #6: Disobedience to Parents

As in the case of blasphemy, we should not be shocked at the rebelliousness of our young when they have watched their parents consume themselves with self-love to a point where the children suffer incalculable damage. There has been for years now a degeneration of respect for anything and every-thing that smacks of order and discipline.

Children watch adults fly in the face of authority in every aspect of life. In sports, adults curse and all but physically attack referees, umpires, and judges—not to mention each other—from the primary level of little league sports and little girl beauty pageants to the big league competitions. Policemen are almost always unjust, unfair, and "stupid cops" when tickets are handed out. And, children are quite obser-vant when road rage strikes while their parent's compete aggressively, even with hostility, against other drivers.

A primary command to parents by God is given by the Apostle Paul in Ephesians 6:4: "Provoke not your children to wrath: but bring them up in the nurture and admonition of the Lord."

Parents who refuse these commands of the Living God risk reaping a bitter harvest of disobedience. We can look around us today and see the terrible consequences of rebellion taking their toll on this generation of young people.

Symptoms #7, #8: Unthankful, Unholy

President Abraham Lincoln officially proclaimed Thanks-giving Day a national holiday in 1863. Thanksgiving, as a concept of thanks for blessings in the land in which we now live, however, was first celebrated in the autumn of 1621, when William Bradford, governor of Plymouth Colony, called for a day of thanksgiving and prayer after the harvest. Other New England colonies gradually adopted the practice.

These godly people, regardless of what revisionist writers of today's accounts of American history claim, escaped England first and foremost for the privilege to worship the one, true God. They knew to whom they were indebted for all blessings they received. Thankfulness and holiness were inseparable in the minds and hearts of our forefathers. They were thankful to the one and only God of Heaven because they sought to be holy and righteous in His omniscient eyes.

How far we have come as a nation and as a world from that 1621 autumn Thanksgiving! People are proud of the things they accumulate, accomplish, attain; they are grateful in some instances to other people and to institutions. For the most part, however, they use the word *thankful* interchangeably with the words *happy* and *pleased,* not in the sense of thankfulness to God.

To be truly thankful to God one must be holy, that is, a believer that God is the provider of all things good. This is a generation of unthankful, unholy people.

Symptom #9: Without Natural Affection
• Abortion

Perhaps no one issue in American society today so fulfills Paul's prophetic end-time characteristic "without natural affection" as does that of abortion. In the great majority of cases in which unborn babies are deliberately exterminated, those doing the killing and those consenting to the murder consider the matter to be no more than medical procedures to solve medical problems.

In most cases, those involved in the abortion process seem to feel no guilt or experience any sorrow over the taking of an unborn child's life. The multiple thousands of victims each year cannot give their views in protest of their impending murders, so they are considered by the abortionists as nothing more than fetal tissue, refuse with which to be done away.

People have been convinced by humanists—the social engineers who claim to want to save planet Earth through human effort, apart totally from God Almighty—that these little ones are not people, that the unborn are not yet human. But the God—whom the humanists in their critical thinking, values clarifying, no-moral-absolutes philosophizing consider to be dead—says something diametrically different. (Read for examples: Jeremiah 1:5; Psalm 103:14; Luke 1:44.)

• Homosexuality

"Without natural affection" also means "unnatural affection." Homosexuality is rampant; sexual deviation and perversion of every sort are looked upon now as private matters between consenting adults.

Sexual deviance, particularly homosexuality, has been the primary benchmark of degeneration at the end of every major empire. Read, for example, Edward Gibbons' *The Decline and Fall of the Roman Empire.* With the court systems of America legislating from the bench the legitimizing of this unnatural activity, can the U.S. be far behind joining the other great nations in the dustbin of history?

Space doesn't allow going into all the other symptoms that characterize end-time mankind. But, some have been covered previously in this study, and some will be touched on later.

Powerful Fuel for the Christian Life!

Everything going on around us points to the fact that we live in a time that exhibits every characteristic about which Paul forewarned. These perilous characteristics, when combined with the other signals given by Old and New Testament prophets, should make any true student of God's prophetic Word sit up and take notice. The Rapture of the saints could be upon us at any moment!

What a powerful excitement this should generate in our hearts to work for the cause of our blessed Lord while there is yet time!

For Additional Study

1. List where Paul's "perilous times" symptoms of end-time man can be found in the Bible.

2. Give an example in our time that resembles Paul's perilous times end-time symptom "fierce."

3. Give examples in our time of people involved in Paul's prophetic symptom "incontinent" (uncontrollably addicted).

4. Give two examples of the end-time symptom "without natural affection" in our time.

5. What is one great commandment addictions violate?

6. What is the greatest commandment, according to Jesus?

7. What does the prophetic Word tell Christians to do when they see all of these end-time signals around them?

8. What is the problem psychology and sociology says lies at the heart of people who commit crimes in many cases?

9. What does God's Word say is at the heart of the problem of all sinners?

Rapture Readiness

KEY PROPHECY POWER TRUTH

"Whatsoever thy hand findeth to do, do it with thy might."

Ecclesiastes 9:10

"Therefore be ye also ready: for in such an hour as ye think not the Son of man cometh."

Matthew 24:44

The Rapture will be a sudden, unannounced event. Millions around the world will vanish in an instant. Clothing and everything worn by each Christian will be left behind wherever it falls. All prosthetic devices, be they glasses, hearing aids, and false eyelashes and fingernails, or whether they be stainless steel hip and knee replacements—all will stay behind.

There will be no need for these earthly things, and, those who are taken will not have to go naked in their new environment. They will be supernaturally clothed. Exactly what each saint will wear is a subject for the next section. The thought for the moment involves the necessity of being always ready for Christ's sudden call: "Come up hither!"

One Electrifying Moment!

Based upon the only Truth there is, and without apology, this lesson is meant to proclaim with absolute confidence the fact that there is indeed coming one electrifying instant in time which will cause changes of epic proportion for all who live upon planet Earth. That event will set in motion massive rearrangements in every facet of human existence. Those rearrangements will ultimately result in what Jesus Himself called the Great Tribulation, a time of trouble far worse than any other in human history.

Jesus Christ, the Living Word (John 1:1, 14), inspired the Apostle Paul to write, "Behold, I show you a mystery; We shall not all sleep, but we shall all be changed, In a moment, in the twinkling of an eye, at the last trump: for the trumpet shall sound, and the dead shall be raised incorruptible, and we shall be changed" (1 Cor. 15:51, 52).

God, the Holy Spirit, further wrote through Paul, "For the Lord himself shall descend from heaven with a shout, with the voice of the archangel, and with the trump of God: and the dead in Christ shall rise first: Then we which are alive and remain shall be caught up together with them in the clouds, to meet the Lord in the air: and so shall we ever be with the Lord. Wherefore comfort one another with these words" (1 Thess. 4:16-18).

Believers Changed Forever

That this will be an electrifying moment for the child of God is perhaps the understatement of understatements! God's Word promises that the body of each believer in Jesus Christ who is alive at the time this indescribably momentous event takes place will be converted in "the twinkling of an eye" from a body that is in the process of decay leading toward death into a body eternally indestructible and beautiful beyond imagination.

The Apostle Paul writes through inspiration: "For this corruptible must put on incorruption, and this mortal must put on immortality. So when this corruptible shall have put on incorruption, and this mortal shall have put on immortality, then shall be brought to pass the saying that is written, Death is swallowed up in victory. O death, where is thy sting? O grave, where is thy victory?" (1 Cor. 15:53, 54).

That instantaneous change from mortal to supernatural being will be exhilarating beyond anything we can imagine within the framework of our present ability to understand.

Face to Face with Jesus

Far exceeding that exhilaration, however, will be the joy of seeing Jesus Christ face to face and at last understanding through transformed and perfected senses the width and height and depth of God's holiness and love. Christians will at last know Christ as He truly is. Each believer will be like Him in that moment and will be eternally in His majestic presence. "But we know that, when he shall appear, we shall be like him; for we shall see him as he is" (1 John 3:2).

The reason for Christ's returning for true believers in Him will be achieved in less than one stunning second! All who have died in Christ will be made ready for heavenly citizenship on the spot, as Jesus Himself promised. The Rapture will include all people who have accepted Him as Savior and Lord.

Christ's Comfort Assured

Jesus promised all who will believe in Him: "Let not your heart be troubled: ye believe in God, believe also in me. In my Father's house are many mansions: if it were not so, I would have told you. I go to prepare a place for you. And if I go and prepare a place for you, I will come again, and receive you unto myself; that where I am, there ye may be also. And whither I go ye know, and the way ye know" (John 14:1-3).

Rapture Will Leave Some All Shook Up

Jesus Christ's sudden catching up of all living believers from the planet's surface, to meet Himself and all believers who have died to begin the journey to the heavenly city where He has been preparing mansions for them, will leave Earth's inhabitants gasping in fear and wonder. That secret taking away of Christ's saints, although termed a mystery by the Apostle Paul (1 Cor. 15:51-58) when he penned the words under the inspiration of the Holy Spirit, needs no longer be a mysterious prophetic doctrine. Truth about this act of God, which will be perhaps the most spectacular of all acts surrounding the greatest of His works—His amazing saving grace through the shed blood of His only begotten Son on the cross at Calvary—has been unveiled for clear understanding in our time.

Daniel's Prophecy in Our Time

The prophet Daniel foretold that as the time for the end of God's plan for the present earth system nears, "knowledge shall be increased" (Dan. 12:4). That knowledge, many biblical scholars believe, while including the vast body of general knowledge, refers most particularly to revealed biblical truths—especially prophetic Truth. When Daniel was told by the angel of God, "Seal the book, even to the time of the end" (Dan. 12:4), it is obvious that God planned to make at least some portion of His mysteries understandable to the generation alive at the end of this present earth system. The discipline of eschatology—the study of end-time matters—is a recent development in the mining of the deep truths of God's prophetic Word.

Book Unsealed?

Has the book Daniel was told would be sealed up until the end now been opened for examination? If so, do the new truths unveiled through eschatological methods as men and women of God are infused with understanding by the Holy Spirit make clear the mystery that Paul wrote about in 1 Corinthians 15:51, 52? He said, "We shall not all sleep, but we shall all be changed in a moment, in the twinkling of an eye." Does any new understanding give credence to any of the several rapture theories?

Unspiritual Spiritualizing

Liberal theologians, almost without exception, proclaim prophecies clearly yet unfulfilled to be spiritual concepts that have already come to pass or spiritual concepts yet to come to pass. They see no physical reality in God's prophetic Word; rather, they consider the prophesied events merely interesting ideas to be used in the exercise of mental gymnastics upon the floor of theological debate.

Unscholarly Scholarship

Tragically, many otherwise fundamentalist, conservative Christian scholars fall into the same trap of rationalizing and/or spiritualizing away future prophetic events such as the 1 Corinthians 15:51-58 description by the Apostle Paul of a stunning event yet to come which he, under inspiration, interpreted to be literal.

Again, without apology, this study is meant to examine the coming microsecond of time in which millions of people will vanish.

Rapture Is Right

The Rapture of all living true believers and the resurrection of the bodies of all believers who have died is a prophecy as Holy Spirit-given as was the prophecy in the Old Testament that promised Jesus Christ's first coming. However, not everyone believes there will be a Rapture. They might believe in space alien abductions, and various otherworldly phenomena such as angelic miracles and supernatural visitations by ghosts, but not something as strange as a Rapture. We've looked at the scoffers in a previous lesson. Let's look, here, at those who do believe that there will be a Rapture. There is by no means total agreement on the subject, even among evangelical Christians who earnestly desire to know the truth held in God's prophetic Word.

The differences in viewpoints can be profound, in that the very character and promises of the Lord God are brought into question. Therefore, it is absolutely essential that you and I look into the matter. It is crucial that we get a grasp of the dif-

---

Be a Berean!

In the final analysis, you must, individually, search the Scriptures for yourself. Don't take this writer's or anyone else's word as the final authority. God's Word is that authority. The Holy Spirit will guide you in your study, while you search the depths of prophecy in the Bible. This is the way to begin getting Rapture ready!

---

ferences, why one viewpoint is correct, and the others are not. This examination must be done carefully, and most of all, scripturally, and prayerfully.

Here are the biblical truths from the viewpoint presented by this study. I believe the views are scripturally correct. Read, study, pray, listen to God's Spirit, then believe God and trust the Lord in complete confidence that He will lead you in His paths (read Proverbs 3:5, 6).

Main Views of the Rapture

1. The Split-Rapture View

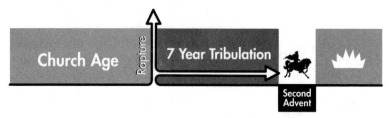

This view holds that only some Christians will be taken in the Rapture. Those taken will be the Christians who have made themselves ready by living holy, righteous lives. All others will have to go through the Tribulation, in order that they purify themselves through the fiery trials of that horrible time.

There are too many problems with this view to delve into the issue very far, but two chief problems are:

- Paul foretells in 1 Corinthians 15:51, 52 that "we all" (believers in Christ) will be changed in a (one, at the same instant) moment, in the "twinkling of an eye." All means "all," not just "some."
- To leave any who were saved would be to require them to again have to make the decision to accept or reject Christ. The earth dwellers during the Tribulation will eventually have to choose between taking Antichrist's mark and refusing that mark. If they take it, they will possibly be able to get food and other things necessary to live, but will be eternally lost, according to God's Word. Thus, Christians would

be subjected to possibly losing their salvation, making security in Jesus void. This would make Jesus a liar.

Saints will not go through any part of the Tribulation!

2. The Mid-Tribulation Rapture View

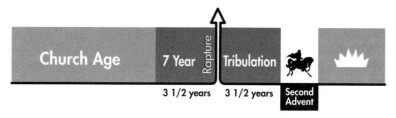

Church Age | 7 Year | Rapture | Tribulation

3 1/2 years | 3 1/2 years | Second Advent

This view, sometimes called the pre-wrath position, is the belief that all Christians will be taken from Earth some time around the middle of the Tribulation. This view holds that God's judgment (His wrath) doesn't begin to fall upon the planet until three and a half years of the Tribulation have passed. This viewpoint doesn't work because God promises: "For God hath not appointed us to wrath, but to obtain salvation by our Lord Jesus Christ. Who died for us, that, whether we wake or sleep, we should live together with him. Wherefore comfort yourselves together, and edify one another, even as also ye do" (1 Thess. 5:9-11).

The Tribulation is seven years of God's wrath falling on people of earth. The mid-trib view claims that only the second half of the seven-year year era is God's wrath, but that's not the truth of the matter. Revelation 6:17 says the time of God's wrath has come. This refers back to Jesus (the Lamb) opening all the seals of God's judgments from the very first seal being broken in Revelation 6:1.

The Mid-Trib view is in error.

3. The Post-Tribulation Rapture View

This viewpoint says that Christians will have to go through the entire seven years of the Tribulation era. The Rapture of the saints will then occur and Christians will join Jesus, who's then on His way back to put a stop to Armageddon.

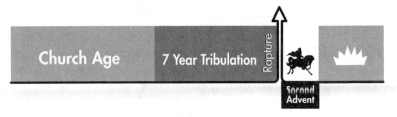

Again, those who hold to the post-trib view believe Christians must go through the terrible seven-year Tribulation era in order to "wash their robes" and make themselves ready for living in Heaven. They confuse the Scriptures in Revelation that say the saints have made themselves ready. That refers to those who are saved during the Tribulation and who have become martyrs for Christ. It has nothing whatever to do with believers who are saved before the Tribulation.

Jesus paid all sin debt on that cruel cross for all who believe. During the dispensation (era) of grace, which is also called the Church Age, there is nothing we can do to be saved—thus secure ourselves against God's wrathful judgment upon sin—but accept Jesus as Savior.

One prime reason the post-trib view is in error is that if all were raptured as Christ is returning to earth to put an end to Armageddon, there would be no mortals (those of blood and flesh) left on earth that are saved. All lost will be judged, then cast into outer darkness, the Bible foretells. The question would be, then: Who would go into the 1,000 years of Christ's reign—the Millennium—to repopulate planet Earth? Immortals neither marry, nor are given in marriage, Jesus said. Marriage was given primarily for the procreation of children. There would be no one to go into the Millennium who could serve this function.

Also, where would the believing remnant of the nation Israel come from if they were raptured as Jesus was returning? If raptured—and they would be raptured as believers— they, too would become immortals, then return. But, there couldn't be a physical, mortal nation that will be the head of all nations, like the Bible plainly prophesies.

4. The Pre-Tribulation Rapture View

This, of course, is the one the Bible teaches. God foretells through Jesus and Paul that before the time of Jacob's trou-

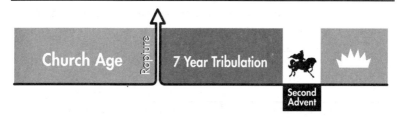

ble (Jeremiah 30:7) begins, Christ will come in the clouds (atmosphere) above earth to call His saints to be with Him forever.

Where other views go wrong is that they fail to recognize the true power of our mighty Lord. He is able to keep us out of the time of Tribulation! (Read Revelation 3:10). Also, those who—sometimes with harsh, condemning criticism—ridicule the Pre-Trib viewpoint, almost without exception, fail to recognize that God's prophetic Word plainly presents two separate programs for dealing with His children. He deals with:

• His chosen people Israel; and
• Gentile Believers in Christ

He handles those groups of people with two separate agendas. Yet these two dovetail into one wonderful, eternal life in Heaven!

How To Get Rapture Ready

That instant leap into Jesus' presence for eternity could literally happen at any second. Let's look at how very near we must be to that stunning event. Also, we must understand what it means to be ready for the Rapture. These thoughts by the late Dr. John Walvoord—in my view the greatest prophecy scholar of modern times—will clue us on these important matters:

> The question remains as to how soon the Rapture will occur. After all, almost two thousand years have passed since this prophecy was given. How does a believer know that there will not be many more years before the Rapture is fulfilled?

The Timing of the Rapture

Many attempts have been made to date the Rapture and all of them have been false because the Bible does not give this information. However, there are indications that the

Rapture could occur very soon. This seems to be a contradiction, because if the Rapture has no signs, how can one say that there are signs of the Rapture approaching.

The answer is found in the sequence of chronological events that occur before the Second Coming. If prophecy is taken literally, the Bible describes in detail exactly what the world situation will be at the Rapture and how events will unfold that finally climax in the Second Coming...

At the time of the Rapture, there apparently will be a revival of the ancient Roman Empire that was in power when Christ was on earth. Today that empire is dead and gone but the Scriptures imply that there will be a resurrection of this empire in the end time. This is indicated in Daniel 7:7-8 where the ten horns of the beast represent ten kingdoms according to Daniel 7:25, and apparently anticipates that there will be revival of the Roman Empire in the form of ten countries. Under these circumstances, it is very significant that developments in the world today seem to pave the way for this...

[It is] clear that we are now for the first time precisely at the moment in history where the Roman Empire could be revived and if this is connected with the rapture of the [saints], it also helps us to date it.

Probably a sensible conclusion is that while the date of the Rapture is not revealed, for the first time, we have some solid evidence that the Rapture could be very soon. This leads to practical conclusions about what we Christians should do in the light of these prophesied events.

Are We Ready for the Rapture?
The reason Christians should be watching for the Rapture rather than the Second Coming is that the Second Coming is not imminent but the Rapture is. If Christ may come any day and Christians who have died will be resurrected and living Christians changed, it obviously puts a challenge before those who are living today to make every day count for Christ. In other words, our opportunities should be maximized in doing the things that we want to do if Christ were coming very soon.

There is no ground in Scripture for frantic efforts, but obviously the first question is are we ready in the sense of are we born again for only Christians who are born again and part of God's family will be raptured. They have to be in Christ [sealed by] the Spirit which occurs at the moment of their faith in Christ. Undoubtedly, many church members will be left behind who fell short of a vital, personal relationship to Jesus Christ.

A second, very practical lesson is that we should be concerned about those around us who are not Christians whether they are loved ones or strangers. Christians should get behind every effort to win people for Christ and they should be engaged in personal evangelism and prayer for the lost, supporting the church and evangelistic efforts in trying to win others to Christ. Certainly, this is a crucial time in history if the Rapture could be very soon.

It should be noted that the Bible does not outline frantic or extreme efforts in preparation for the Lord's return. The Bible does not indicate that Christians should give all their money away as some have tried to do who have dated the Rapture. Instead, however, Christians should be wise stewards giving as much as they can because obviously if the Rapture occurs, they will leave behind whatever physical wealth they have. It is also obvious that we have many opportunities for service for God in recognition of His plan and program and we should order our lives especially as they are related to eternal values, things that will really count as we stand before Christ, the judgment seat of rewards, which the Bible describes as following the Rapture. Accordingly, we watch because it could be soon but watching is not enough. We must be serving and making the most of our remaining time (—excerpt from Dr. Walvoord's chapter, "Why We Watch," in William T. James' book, *Raging into Apocalypse: Essays in Apocalypse IV* (New Leaf Press: Green Forest, AR, pages 266-269.)

For Additional Study

1. What will raptured Christians leave behind?

2. What are the two primary passages that teach the Rapture?

3. What will happen to those alive when the Rapture happens?

4. What will happen to the bodies of those saints who have died?

5. How long will the raptured saints remain with Jesus?

6. Who will be raptured?

7. Where will Jesus and His saints go from the air above earth?

8. Where are the Scriptures containing this prophetic promise?

9. What does the word "eschatology" mean?

10. Where is the prophecy that many prophetic things will be sealed from being known until the very end-time?

11. List the four main Rapture views.

Planet Earth Throws a Party!

KEY PROPHECY POWER TRUTH

"And for this cause God shall send them strong delusion, that they should believe a lie."

2 Thessalonians 2:11

Ever feel like things are falling apart around you? Not only in your personal life, but in your town, your state, your nation, your world? Well, things are, in fact, falling apart. This is due to sin, which infects and affects everything.

Universal Yearning

Most everyone yearns for a time of peace and plenty. Things aren't getting better and better like the evolutionists proclaim. We are not evolving to some sort of super-human existence, the way New Agers would have us believe. Things are degenerating, just as Bible prophecy foretells. But, there is a day coming when the brilliant dawn of the Bright and Morning Star will break upon this war-torn, sin-infected planet. His name is Jesus, and He will one day reverse the downward spiral humanity is experiencing.

False Fulfillment

First, however, there will come a false sense that Utopia has arrived. The "man of sin," Antichrist, will fool people by the millions, promising that Heaven has come to Earth. It will be all promise, however, and little peace will be produced. The great leader's promises will prove even emptier than the promises given by some of today's politicians. And, the false promises will be infinitely more dangerous. Nonetheless, gullible inhabitants of Earth, tired of their pain filled, chaotic world, will clamor to jump on the great leader's bandwagon of prosperity and plenty. When the Christians are no longer here to point condemning fingers—to hold them back in their progress toward producing Heaven on Earth—they will have a planet Earth party, no doubt. At one point, they will send notes of congratulations to each other, that now they can do as they please, uninhibited by guilt. They will do what is right in their own eyes.

Paul the Apostle said this end-time party was already in the planning stages during his time: "For the mystery of iniquity doth already work: only he who now letteth will let, until he be taken out of the way. And then shall that Wicked be revealed, whom the Lord shall consume with the spirit of his mouth, and shall destroy with the brightness of his coming: Even him, whose coming is after the working of Satan with all power and signs and lying wonders, And with all deceivableness of unrighteousness in them that perish; because they received not the love of the truth, that they might be saved. And for this cause God shall send them strong delusion, that they should believe a lie: That they all might be damned who believed not the truth, but had pleasure in unrighteousness" (2 Thess. 2:7-12).

Crying Out for Peace and Safety

Practically every indicator within the scope of human affairs points to restlessness, turmoil, and to wars and rumors of wars. Jesus' words as recorded in Matthew 24:5-8 could easily be applied to our times. The Lord said in that account, "For many shall come in my name, saying, I am Christ; and shall deceive many. And ye shall hear of wars and rumors of wars; see that ye be not troubled: for all these things must come to pass, but the end is not yet. For nation shall rise against nation, and kingdom against kingdom; and there shall be famines, and pestilences, and earthquakes, in divers places. All these are the beginning of sorrows."

No Peace in Our Time

Although Jesus was referring specifically to the Tribulation Period, that seven-year period of apocalypse which will conclude with His Second Advent at the time of Armageddon, He also said in Luke 21:28 that "when these things begin to come to pass" we are to "look up, and lift up [our] heads; for our redemption draweth near." Jesus said that these indicators would be "the beginning of sorrows," or birth pangs.

End-Time Indicators

The Lord warned that these symptoms of the end time will increase in frequency and intensity as the time of His return approaches like the labor contractions a woman suffers when the birth of her child nears. His words seemed to emphasize that man's rebelliousness and wickedness will again be at levels like in the days of Noah and the days of Lot (Luke 17:26-30). Mankind's incorrigible rebelliousness will bring God's wrath.

Global Outcry

Certainly, this generation cries out for peace. Most conspicuous in this regard is the global outcry for a cessation of hostilities between Israel and its Palestinian neighbors. The hue and cry for peace, however, can be heard from every quarter on Earth. From nations in conflict with each other, from ethnic groups warring one against another, from communities experiencing ever increasing violence, from families in turmoil, from individuals who murder and maim each other, every hour of every day, they cry "peace, peace! when there is no peace" (Jer. 6:14; 8:11).

Any Solution but God

This generation seeks to calm the rage, but does so through anything and everything but the one and only source of true peace, Jesus Christ. The poorest among our number seek comfort, solace and sustenance from governmental bureaucracies. The middle class seeks to keep noses above the flood of taxes those bureaucracies issue forth. Yet at the same time, the middle class gropes for temporal pleasures, entertainment, and material goods that might provide moments of peace that never seem to come. The wealthy and elite grasp for satisfaction they perceive as attainable through the pursuit of money, power and self-aggrandizement.

Anybody but God

Idolatry of every sort rules throughout every strata of every culture and society today. God is pushed farther and farther from the thoughts of men who seek only to praise their gods of this age.

Humanism's Failure

Humanistic efforts inevitably fail. Fires of discontent are the result of man's refusal to give God the praise and worship He alone deserves. That fire will soon produce seven years of hell on Earth. As Jesus warned the Pharisees, "The very stones will cry out."

Preparing for the Party

People, when they believe that all of these troubles will be put behind them, will doubtless whip themselves into a party mood. To understand what the big Earth Party will be like shortly after the Rapture takes place, we must look at the preparations for that time of great celebration during the present day.

Profiles in Prophecy

Bible prophecy foretells the Rapture and the times and people the saints will leave behind in the following verses: "The Lord knoweth how to deliver the godly out of temptations, and to reserve the unjust unto the day of judgment to be punished: But chiefly them that walk after the flesh in the lust of uncleanness, and despise government. Presumptuous are they, selfwilled, they are not afraid to speak evil of dignities. . . . But these, as natural brute beasts, made to be taken and destroyed, speak evil of the things that they understand not; and shall utterly perish in their own corruption; And shall receive the reward of unrighteousness, as they that count it pleasure to riot in the day time. Spots they are and blemishes, sporting themselves with their own deceivings . . . Having eyes full of adultery, and that cannot cease from sin; beguiling unstable souls: an heart they have exercised with covetous practices; cursed children: Which have forsaken the right way, and are gone astray, . . . These are wells without water, clouds that are carried with a tempest; to whom the mist of darkness is reserved for ever. For it had been better for them not to have known the way of righteousness than, after they have known it, to turn from the holy commandment delivered unto them" (2 Peter 2:9, 10, 12, 13, 14, 15, 17, 21).

Defying God and Forefathers

America's founding fathers determined to set this nation upon a foundation of God-given principles. Yet one federal judge can command that those godly principles, the Ten Commandments, be removed from a schoolhouse or courtroom wall. The Supreme Court of the land can declare God's Word null and void and His Son, Jesus Christ, a nondesirable entity by declaring Christianity too narrow and bigoted to be presented within America's educational process alongside pagan deities and pagan forms of worship which, in many cases, have governmental approval. The results of such foolhardiness are inevitable.

Worse Than Genocide

This disregard for God's Truth is disregard for life. Such disregard is, in some sense, worse than atrocities committed by those we consider barbarians in regions that have not been so blessed by God as ours. Jesus Christ is the Way, the Truth, and the Life (John 14:6). To reject and blaspheme the only begotten Son of God is to display the ultimate disregard for life. Rejecting Jesus Christ, the Prince of Peace, brings the opposite of peace—chaos and war.

War in the Home

Humanism, the system embodying man's determination to construct the world in his own image totally apart from God's authority, is making an indelible imprint upon American family life. Homes are ripped apart by selfish actions that cast aside the notion of personal responsibility.

The Evolution Generation

A generation has arisen from the chaos of evolution-based education. Man is but the highest evolved form of animal life, the hellish doctrine goes, and, like the lower animals, has needs that supersede any obligation to some nebulous concept of morality.

Hollywood's Insidious Influences

Hollywood portrays the supposedly liberated man or woman as a sexual creature not unlike a dog in the street who can simply mate on the spur of the moment, then separate after having satisfied their primal urges. There are no consequences, only self-satisfaction and contentment until the next primal urge wells within.

Sexual innuendo and outright reference are every-night fare on sit-coms and regular TV programming. It's just good fun, the defenders offer when critics speak out. There is no real harm, they proclaim. Yet many who create the sexually oriented programs are among those who cry the loudest in the fight against sexual harassment in the military, in business, and in society. This sort of convoluted reasoning—that it is okay to program the minds of men with scenes of sexual debauchery in the name of "fun" entertainment but it is not okay for these same programmed men to put their fantasies into action by assaulting women in the workplace—God's Word calls reprobate thinking.

Animal-Like Activity

Growing numbers of men are following the "if it feels good, do it" tenets taught by humanism and vividly portrayed by Hollywood. Divorce rates continue to climb, the majority of them due to men leaving wives and children to pursue relationships that require of them little or no responsibility.

Sexual predators are the ultimate product of this "if it feels good, do it" preprogramming by entertainment media, and by pornographers now on Internet. These people sometimes end up serial rapists and/or murderers. Men are almost always the predators who seek out their victims for their evil gratification. In a way, these predators are, themselves, victims— victimized by those who are just making it so people can be entertained by spoofing human sexuality. This is not to say that women are not culpable as well. Statistics show a growing number of women deserting husbands and children for the same self-centered reasons.

Marriage Marginalized

Why get married? That is another attitude that pervades American culture today. Single mothers who have never been married constitute a rising tide of irresponsible behavior that portends great trouble in the near future. Gangs of youth without fathers to nurture and discipline them cling to each other and rage against a society that neither understands nor seems to care except when crimes committed by the gang members on occasion directly touch our lives.

Murder in the Womb

Abortion proponents give unwanted children (such as those who end up in gangs and who might predictably produce future gang members) as good reasons for ending pregnancies. Such children, if allowed to be born, they say, will only suffer the abuse of America's gang culture or worse. The truth is, however, that abortion imprints upon the minds of our children the idea that human life is a commodity like any other commodity and can be discarded without a second thought. Man, not God, it is implied, has authority over life and death. The message clearly has gotten through to the young gang members who slaughter each other each night across America.

The millions, even billions of people who will be left behind when the Rapture occurs, will have been prepared for the Tribulation era "Earth Party." If they resent being restrained now, imagine what many will be like in that time when they are not under the influence of restraint God's Holy Spirit formerly provided.

Antichrist's "Peace"

Satan's "man of sin" will convince people of earth that they can have their cake and eat it too, to use a well-worn cliché. He will promise they can do whatever they wish, free of guilt that they are breaking some god's commandment. Yet, he will at the same time guarantee them complete freedom from fear that the chaos of former times will ever again bedevil their lives. He will convince one and all that he will build—with their cooperation—"Heaven on Earth!"

Fear caused by the disappearance of millions around the world will no doubt change to glee that now they have a fresh start. They will build a world of their own choosing. The party will begin!

Delusions of Grandeur

The world's great one-world thinkers and planners, led more and more by the man who will quickly become known as the greatest of all time, will come up with spectacular ideas to create the new world order.

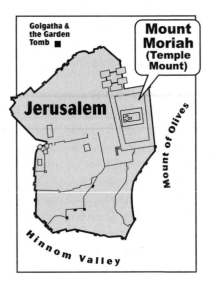

Part of that grandiose plan probably will include a peace plan that neither the Jews of Israel nor Israel's blood-vowed enemies will be able to refuse. Included in that plan will most likely be giving Jews permission to build a temple atop Mount Moriah.

Ingredients of the Great Plan

The plan will probably include a complete redistribution of wealth. Possibly, all the properties of those who vanished will be pooled, then divided and distributed within nations, and across the world.

Everyone will likely have access to computer usage, eventually. Thus to be able to conduct business over the hybrid Internet system that will probably grow at a fantastic rate. The greatest part of this phenomenal system most likely will be the ability of each person to cast their vote on leaders and issues electronically. A true world democracy at last achieved. What the people won't know, however, will be that their voting decisions will be manipulated to show results the grand schemer's desire.

Man Creates Wrath from God

Perhaps the most ironic judgment of all will be wrapped up in the fact that mankind will be allowed to do things its way, basically apart from God's influence. The people, themselves, will create their own hell on Earth. But, still, this God-free society will be as much a judgment from the Almighty as will be the judgments of the second half of the Tribulation, when God pours His increasingly terrible vengeance upon rebellious earth-dwellers.

It will be a worldwide "Earth Party" of short duration. At the midway point of the seven-year Tribulation, the great world leader will prove what and who he really is! We will look at that horrendous future era in a following lesson. For now, let's close on a majestic note concerning the power that is in God's prophetic program. Dr. Dave Breese, one of my dearest friends, who went to be with the Lord in 2002, will do the honors. Dave wrote in his masterfully eloquent style:

The Glory to Come

Let each of us be finally reminded that the story of the future is not simply that of one day after another ad infinitum. No indeed! There is a glorious future for [saints], and there is a dismal future for the world. The sojourn of [Christians] in this world will come to an instantaneous end, at which time every believer will be taken from this dark planet to the glory which is to come.

At the moment of that transition, each of us will receive a new body, a glorified body that is not unlike the body of Christ himself. We will at this point be given the capacity to feel, to appreciate, to enjoy all of the unspeakably wonderful things that will be ours in eternity. The Scripture says, In thy presence is fullness of joy; at thy right hand there are pleasures for evermore (Psalm 16:11).

So great will be the delights of heaven that they are impossible to describe under the constraints, the limitations of human language. It may, therefore, be well to exercise a sanctified imagination, to ask the question, What will it be like when Jesus comes? The answer, of course, is that it will be like nothing we can imagine in all of life. There is no human experience that resembles in any but the palest fashion the ecstasy that will be ours when we step across the great divide into the fadeless light of Heaven.

What is Heaven like? The answer must be that Heaven is not exactly like anything that we know in this world. We do well to take the greatest joys of earth and multiply them by a thousand times. Only then do we have even the beginning of the joys that will be ours in Heaven.

The Christian is invited to use his 'sanctified imagination' to think of golden streets, ivory palaces, a city where there is no night, and endless 'pleasure forevermore.' In Heaven also, we will have the opportunity to meet the saints who have gone before and, of course, loved ones who have in earlier days moved from the [saints] militant to the [saints] triumphant. How wonderful to contemplate that golden moment when [believers] will be translated from this world to the world to come. What a moment that will be!

The real point is that we be prepared for that moment. The preparation is that we must be Christians. A Christian is one who believes the gospel of Jesus Christ, who has accepted the Son of the living God as personal Savior. Because of the shed blood of Jesus Christ, the sufficient sacrifice for sin, each person in all of the world is invited to receive the free gift, the gift of God, which is everlasting life. The single requirement is faith alone. By believing in Jesus Christ—who He was and what He did for man on the cross—by that act of faith I receive the gift of God, which is life eternal.

Meanwhile, in these days, let us gather together at the cross, recognizing Jesus Christ as the Savior whose sacrifice made eternal life possible. While laboring for Him here, let us also anticipate the sound of the trumpet when we will be caught up to be with Him (Dave Breese's chapter, "The Rapture," in William T. James' book, *Storming Toward Armageddon, Essays in Apocalypse* (New Leaf Press: Green Forest, AR, 1992, p. 319-320).

For Additional Study

1. Why are things falling apart in the world—that is: Why are things getting worse, not better?

2. How will this downward spiral be stopped?

3. Who will come offering false hope, before Christ's Second Advent?

4. Who is "he who now letteth will let, until he be taken out of the way" of 2 Thessalonians 2:7?

5. What did Jesus forewarn signs of the end-time would be like as the very last days approach?

6. What other times in history did Jesus say the very end of the age would closely resemble?

7. What is the most prominent signal that our generation is near the end of the age?

8. What is humanism, and what's wrong with it?

9. What will God do that will be an ironic judgment in the first half of the Tribulation?

This Is Your Life!

KEY PROPHECY POWER TRUTH

"For we must all appear before the judgment seat of Christ; that every one may receive the things done in his body, according to that he hath done, whether it be good or bad."

2 Corinthians 5:10

We who are of a certain generation remember a TV show in the late 1950s called "This is Your Life!" Each week the host, Ralph Edwards, would come on the air, whispering, usually holding a large book under one arm, and a microphone in the other. He would look directly at us through our black and white TV screens and then glance nervously around him while the camera panned from him, to see if it could locate the guest of honor for the evening's program.

Finally, someone would walk into the bright glare of the television spotlights on some sidewalk in New York, or elsewhere. That person would have another person in tow, and would tug him toward Ralph Edwards.

The person in tow would appear to be greatly surprised, his mouth and eyes widening in disbelief when he realized he had been tricked into coming to the spot so "This is Your Life!" could spend the next 30 minutes—minus commercials—going over his life for the TV viewers.

Our Turn Is Coming!

We who are Christians have a review of our lives coming that will be much greater in scope than the biographies that Ralph Edwards did on any of the celebrities he reviewed for many years. Not one moment of our lives will be missed by our Reviewer because the One who will review our lives from start to finish will be none other than the Lord Jesus, Himself!

We will look in this lesson, of course, at the Judgment Seat of Christ, and all it will encompass. Only the saved will be at this judgment, which is not a judgment for sins committed, but a judgment that will be for determining our eternal rewards.

All About the Bema

Have you ever thought about how it will be on Judgment Day? Many think that when that day comes, everybody will stand in a long line, perhaps one that will circle the Earth many times.

The thought seems to be that we will all wait our turn. When our name is finally called, we will approach the throne, where an angry looking old man with white hair, his eyes on fire, a scowl on his face, will say something like: "Let's have a look at how bad you've been, and whether you've done anything good at all."

An angel, or someone, will come from somewhere, carrying a large balance scale. Somehow, using some sort of measure, our good deeds will be put on one side of the scale. Our bad deeds will be placed on the other side.

Depending upon whether the scale dips toward the "good" side, or the "bad" side, will determine our eternal fate. If we've done more good than bad we go to Heaven. If it tilts the other way we go to . . . well, you know that result . . . No one seems to consider what might happen if things balance perfectly.

No Fairy Tale

As one prophecy teacher I know says: "You'll find that description of Judgment Day in the Bible in the same place you'll find the story of Rudolph the red-nosed reindeer." Sadly, there are far too many Christians who have no more idea of what God's review of their lives will be like, than that described above. This study is meant to help us understand, as thoroughly as God's Word allows, what one of the major judgments following life on this planet, will be like.

Supreme Court Appearance

Each person who has ever been born has a destiny that includes standing before Almighty God. There's no escaping it. You and I will stand before the one, true God, the Creator of all things. The writer of Hebrews tells us: "it is appointed unto men once to die, but after this the judgment" (Heb. 9:27). Make no mistake, we will one day stand before the Supreme Court!

Two Judgments Await

Not only will there not be one long line, where we stand in dread for a few thousand years awaiting our turns, there will not be one judgment, but two. The first judgment to take place will be the Bema Judgment, also called the "Judgment Seat of Christ." The second, the final judgment, will be the "Great White Throne Judgment." You do not want to be at the second of these two judgments—not unless you are there as witness to God's righteousness, rather than as one who is being judged. You definitely want to be at the first, however. The reason this is so is because only the saved stand before Christ at the first judgment, and only the lost stand before God at the second. Everyone at the first judgment will go into Heaven to live eternally in God's presence. Everyone who stands before God in the second judgment will go into hell, apart from God for eternity.

We will look at the Judgment Seat of Christ for now, to get a handle on exactly what Bible prophecy says awaits each of us who name the name of Jesus in the intimate way essential for salvation.

For Supernatural Athletes Only!

Have you ever admired a great athlete, and wished you had that kind of ability? The super athletes of our time make the big bucks, garner great attention, and seem to thrive with rewards of their tremendous feats.

God's Word tells us that we are competing in a contest that is supernatural, and that has eternal consequences. All who are on God's team are expected to give it their very best effort in this great race we call life. Paul the apostle likens our competition to a number of athletic events. The analogy is to the competitions of the Olympic games of ancient times.

Christians are in competition that involves far more profound consequences than do the athletic feats accomplished by even the world's greatest athletes in earthly sports events. The competition is with ourselves. It is individual. We should strive to achieve our utmost potential in order to give honor and glory to our Lord Jesus Christ, by whom and for whom we were made.

Paul Was a Real Sport

Paul was a man of many facets, not just some guy walking around spouting pious things. He was a tremendous scholar, a great missionary and evangelist, and a tentmaker. He was also a terrific sports fan. We know from his writings that Paul was indeed a fellow who followed the athletic competitions of his day with great relish. He used analogies and allusions to sport terms in his instructions on how God wants us to live. He refers in the following to such a sports analogy: "Wherefore seeing we also are compassed about with so great a cloud of witnesses, let us lay aside every weight, and the sin which doth so easily beset us, and let us run with patience the race that is set before us, Looking unto Jesus the author and finisher of our faith; who for the joy that was set before him endured the cross, despising the shame, and is set down at the right hand of the throne of God" (Heb. 12:1, 2).

Bema Background

Paul based much of his sports analogy on his knowledge of the Bema of athletic competitions of his day. One writer clues us to what Paul was talking about in this analogy. "In the large Olympic arenas there was an elevated seat on which the judge of the contest sat. After the contests were over, the successful competitors would assemble before the Bema to receive their rewards or crowns. The Bema was not a judicial bench where someone was condemned. It was a reward seat. Likewise, the Judgment Seat of Christ is not a judicial bench. The Christian life is a race, and the Divine umpire is watching every contestant. After the [saints have] run [their] course, He will gather [them] before the Bema for the purpose of examining each one, and giving the proper reward to each" (Levin Strauss, *God's Plan for the Future,* Zondervan, p.111).

Paul Pleased

The great apostle indicated that at the end of his own life he was satisfied he had given all he had for his Lord, who is also his Judge. "For I am now ready to be offered, and the time of my departure is at hand. I have fought a good fight, I have finished my course, I have kept the faith: Henceforth there is laid up for me a crown of righteousness, which the Lord, the righteous judge, shall give me at that day: and not to me only, but unto all them also that love his appearing" (2 Tim. 4:6-8).

How thrilling! Did you catch that?

Paul says in this prophecy that not only he, but we who run the race with all we have will also receive great rewards. But he says more than that. He prophesies that there is a special reward for Christians who "love his [Jesus'] appearing." Now that's an empowering truth for those who look for the Lord Jesus at any moment in the Rapture!

Building Before the Bema

A person, at the moment he accepts Christ, is instantly placed upon a rock-solid foundation. The Truth of that foundation is found in the following: "He saith unto them, But whom say ye that I am? And Simon Peter answered and said, Thou art the Christ, the Son of the living God. And Jesus answered and said unto him, Blessed art thou, Simon Bar-jona: for flesh and blood hath not revealed it unto thee, but my Father which is in heaven. And I say also unto thee, That thou art Peter, and upon this rock I will build my church; and the gates of hell shall not prevail against it" (Matt. 16:15-18).

Jesus, Our Rock!

Jesus was not saying here that Peter was the rock upon which His church would be built, but that Jesus is that Rock. This foundation stone is the same stone that will smash all anti-God, Antichrist humanistic government at Christ's Second Coming (Dan. 2:34, 35).

Paul says about Jesus, the foundation: "For other foundation can no man lay than that is laid, which is Jesus Christ" (1 Cor. 3:11).

Beware of Error

Some teach the error that we must work to earn and maintain our salvation. The Scriptures above plainly teach otherwise. There is no other foundation whereby we can become God's children: "Neither is there salvation in any other: for there is none other name under heaven given among men, whereby we must be saved" (Acts 4:12).

So, our immortal souls can never be in danger of facing God's wrath, once we are upon the foundation, which is His blessed Son, Jesus. Nonetheless, our eternal destiny is still subject to influence, based upon how we live our lives while still in this realm of earthly existence.

You see, we, when we are set upon that unshakable foundation—the Lord Jesus Christ—we immediately begin building on that solid Rock. We send the materials ahead of our trip to glory—whether that trip be through death or the Rapture—for constructing our eternal dwelling place and for making our heavenly wardrobe. In that sense, our works while in this life do affect our eternal destiny.

Building Supplies Tested

The building materials we send ahead in the form of our works on this earth will have to pass God's test to determine their worthiness for heavenly construction. The testing will take place at the Bema—the Judgment Seat of Christ. Here's what God's Word has to say about that moment of testing for each of us: "For we are labourers together with God: ye are God's husbandry, ye are God's building. According to the grace of God which is given unto me, as a wise masterbuilder, I have laid the foundation, and another buildeth thereon. But let every man take heed how he buildeth thereupon. For other foundation can no man lay than that is laid, which is Jesus Christ. Now if any man build upon this foundation gold, silver, precious stones, wood, hay, stubble; Every man's work shall be made manifest: for the day shall declare it, because it shall be revealed by fire; and the fire shall try every man's work of what sort it is" (1 Cor. 3:9-13).

Salvation Secure for Eternity

Paul, under divine inspiration, is quick to tell us that this judgment in no way will determine whether the person being judged is allowed to enter Heaven. The one being judged is eternally secure from the very moment of salvation. Paul writes about the Bema Judgment further: "If any man's work abide which he hath built thereupon, he shall receive a reward. If any man's work shall be burned, he shall suffer loss: but he himself shall be saved; yet so as by fire" (1 Cor. 3:14, 15).

Our True Reward

We must each stand before the Judgment Seat of Christ to give an account of what we did while living on earth. We will either receive rewards or suffer loss of rewards. The good works we do in the sight of God are symbolized as made of gold, silver, and precious stones. Our worthless works are represented as wood, stubble and hay.

Heavenly fire of righteousness will be applied to each work we did in life while we stand before the Bema. The gold, silver and precious stones will stand the test by fire, and all dross (useless, excess) will burn off. Only the pure, refined works will remain. All other works will perish in the heavenly fire.

Again, this has nothing to do with salvation of our souls. That was settled the moment we accepted Jesus as Savior, while still in physical life on earth. Jesus will then bestow upon each believer his rewards, based upon the refined gold, silver and precious stone works that have been tested in the fires of supreme Judgment.

Greatest Reward of All

The greatest reward of all will be to hear our Lord say to us the same thing the master said to his servant in the story Jesus told while teaching. "His lord said unto him, Well done, thou good and faithful servant: thou hast been faithful over a few things, I will make thee ruler over many things: enter thou into the joy of thy lord" (Matt. 25:21).

Which Works Are Which?

Although it's not easy to know exactly what goes into making a gold, silver, and precious stone work, or a wood, hay, and stubble work, God's Word informs us about certain, general areas of life where God is particularly interested.

We will look scripturally and in-depth in Lesson 12 at the crowns that will be given at the Bema. We will, with equal scriptural intensity, look in Lesson 13 at the areas of living life on earth in which the Christian will be tested at the Judgment Seat of Christ.

For now, it is the greatest banquet that will ever be held that takes stage-center in God's Prophetic Program.

The Marriage Supper of the Lamb

What a contrast this banquet will be to the feast-taking place on planet Earth!

A Grisly Dinner

We read about that grotesque earthly banquet: "And I saw an angel standing in the sun; and he cried with a loud voice, saying to all the fowls that fly in the midst of heaven, Come and gather yourselves together unto the supper of the great God; That ye may eat the flesh of kings, and the flesh of captains, and the flesh of mighty men, and the flesh of horses, and of them that sit on them, and the flesh of all men, both free and bond, both small and great. And I saw the beast, and the kings of the earth, and their armies, gathered together to make war against him that sat on the horse, and against his army. And the beast was taken, and with him the false prophet that wrought miracles before him, with which he deceived them that had received the mark of the beast, and them that worshipped his image. These both were cast alive into a lake of fire burning with brimstone. And the remnant were slain with the sword of him that sat upon the horse, which sword proceeded out of his mouth: and all the fowls were filled with their flesh" (Rev. 19:17-21).

The human carnage will be stupendous. But it will be righteous judgment that is well deserved. The carrion of earth will indeed have their fill!

The Most Extravagant Wedding Feast Ever

The Church Age saints of God whom the Bible says have white robes of righteousness will be the wife of the Lamb (Jesus Christ). This is the bride the Apostle Paul wrote about as follows: "Husbands, love your wives, even as Christ also loved the church, and gave himself for it; That he might sanctify and cleanse it with the washing of water by the word, That he might present it to himself a glorious church, not having spot, or wrinkle, or any such thing; but that it should be holy and without blemish. So ought men to love their wives as their own bodies. He that loveth his wife loveth himself. For no man ever yet hated his own flesh; but nourisheth and cherisheth it, even as the Lord the church: For we are members of his body, of his flesh, and of his bones. For this cause shall a man leave his father and mother, and shall be joined unto his wife, and they two shall be one flesh. This is a great mystery: but I speak concerning Christ and the church" (Eph. 5:25-32).

A number of views on exactly whom the bride will be has been a cause for debate. The purpose here is to present what God's Word says, advising each child of God to study, pray and seek Holy Spirit direction while considering this awesome topic of prophecy yet future. The Scripture on the Marriage Supper of the Lamb we are given, specifically, says: "Let us be glad and rejoice, and give honour to him: for the marriage of the Lamb is come, and his wife hath made herself ready. And to her was granted that she should be arrayed in fine linen, clean and white: for the fine linen is the righteousness of saints. And he saith unto me, Write, Blessed are they which are called unto the marriage supper of the Lamb. And he saith unto me, These are the true sayings of God" (Rev. 19:7-9).

The bride will forever be with her Lord, the King of all kings. All saints of all ages will have different duties to perform and offices to administrate, but the body of believers who constitute the Bride of Christ will be with Him forever in a special relationship, while serving Him as He wills, based upon Bema rewards earned while during earthly life.

For Additional Study

1. Who will examine believers' lives at the Bema or Judgment Seat of Christ?

2. What is the purpose of the Bema?

3. Are sins examined at the Bema?

4. Name the two Judgments, and define each.

5. With whom do we compete as Christians, as we run the race before us?

6. What was Paul's Bema seat sport's analogy based upon in instructing on how to run the race of life?

7. What is the rock upon which Jesus said He will build His Church?

8. Give another example, in prophecy, that portrays Jesus as a rock.

9. What are we as Christians to do with the foundation stone Jesus talked about?

10. List the six building materials that will be tried by fire at the Bema.

11. What will be the greatest reward we can get?

12. What will Christians do with the crowns they have earned, when the Bema examination is finished?

Party's Over!

KEY PROPHECY POWER TRUTH

"For then shall be great tribulation, such as was not since the beginning of the world to this time, no, nor ever shall be."

Matthew 24:21

Planet Earth, as we have seen, will throw a party of sorts following Christ's saints Rapture into Heaven. Earth-dwellers will be deluded into thinking, at some point, that the evil or hindering influences that have held progress back have been removed. Now they can have their Utopian existence on this planet. That thought will be at the heart of their jubilation. Their frenzied elation will soon turn to uncertainty, then fear, then to terror beyond ability to describe. Their existence will turn into hell on earth.

God's Cup of Wrath Overflows

God's cup of judgment has been filling since the time He poured it out the first time. That first time was the Flood that covered the whole earth, when only Noah and seven of his family members went into the ark, and God, Himself, shut and sealed the door.

His saints (Noah and his family) rose above the judgment—were saved out of the carnage in which everything that lived on the earth's land died.

Saints Will Rise!

One day—perhaps today—God's saints will be taken from the planet's surface, and, ultimately, God's judgment will again flood the earth. Billions will die in the judgment, but they will not die from a flood of waters. It will be a deluge of 21 specific judgments, which God's Word describes as being sent in a three-part series:

1. Scrolls
2. Trumpets
3. Vials (bowls)

Seven judgments will be coming from each of the series. We will study these terrible, though righteous and necessary judgments in some detail in the next lesson.

Twofold Purpose of Judgments

Earth's party won't get too far into the celebrations before things will begin to go wrong—terribly wrong. The great world leader will step to the forefront and offer a plan that will astound the people of the planet. Peace between Israel and its hatred-filled, blood-vowed enemies will be at the heart of the great man's blueprint for beginning again, planet Earth's drive toward Heaven on earth.

Peace That Destroys

But, the peace that the leader assures by signing the covenant that guarantees Israel's security will be the very thing that fills God's cup of wrath to overflowing. Israel's acceptance of Antichrist, having rejected Jesus Christ, their Messiah, at least two millennia earlier, will cause God's fury to become full-blown. Jesus Himself said of Israel's rejection, and of that future time when Israel will accept Antichrist: "I am come in my Father's name, and ye receive me not: if another shall come in his own name, him ye will receive" (John 5:43).

God's anger will flow in increasing volume upon the inhabitants of earth who will not turn from their sin against Him. Daniel, the great prophet, prophesied the whole end-time scenario, from the time Israel rejected their Messiah, through the very end of the terrible time of God's judgments that will end the Tribulation and bring Christ's Second coming in power and glory. "And after threescore and two weeks shall Messiah be cut off, but not for himself: and the people of the prince that shall come shall destroy the city and the sanctuary; and the end thereof shall be with a flood, and unto the end of the war desolations are determined. And he shall confirm the covenant with many for one week: and in the midst of the week he shall cause the sacrifice and the oblation to cease, and for the overspreading of abominations he shall make it desolate, even until the consummation, and that determined shall be poured upon the desolate" (Dan. 9:26, 27).

Purpose Behind Judgments

The purpose of these righteous judgments—for the whole of Daniel's seventieth week, the Tribulation—are twofold:

1) to purge out a remnant of Israel to love and obey God and be His people forever
2) to bring a vast number of people out of the Gentile world to be His people for eternity

Purging Israel

The first purpose in God sending judgment upon the earth once Antichrist confirms the covenant of security (peace) will be to call out a remnant of His chosen people, the Jews, as a people who love Him, and will obey Him. Dr. Dave Breese presents this process in the following.

The Time of Jacob's Trouble

The Tribulation is, therefore, the time of Jacob's trouble. Jeremiah says, "Alas! for that day is great, so that none is like it: it is even the time of Jacob's trouble; but he shall be saved out of it" (Jer. 30:7).

Israel is held responsible by the Lord, along with the Gentiles, for the crucifixion of Christ. This is the reason for the awesome silence of Jehovah in relating to His people during the two millennia that have transpired since the death of Christ. Clearly, however, the Word of God declares that God has not finally and completely cast away His people.

Indeed, the Scripture speaks of the casting away of Israel and announced that that [casting away] produced the reconciling of the world. The Scripture then speaks of the receiving of Israel, which will be life from the dead for the nations. Israel moved into a period of blindness and estrangement from God until a point of time called the fullness of the Gentiles (Rom. 11:25).

At this point, God promises to work in goodness and severity with His people so that . . . Israel will be brought to a place of decision and faith. This is always the intention of divine discipline for His own, in any era of history.

The Tribulation, then, will be a time of the conversion of Israel. Most boldly, the Scripture announces, "And so all Israel shall be saved: as it is written, There shall come out of Zion the Deliverer, and shall turn away ungodliness from Jacob; For this is my covenant unto them, when I shall take away their sins" (Rom. 11:26-27) (Breese, "The Rapture," *Storming Toward Armageddon,* p. 296).

Spiritual Revival

The Tribulation will, therefore, be a time of great spiritual revival. It will mark the conversion of Israel and great activity by Israel for the conversion of the world. The Book of Revelation, therefore, announces an amazing multitude of 144,000 witnesses who represent the twelve tribes of Israel. These will have been converted during the days of the Tribulation and will have a profound effect upon the world. When one remembers that there is only a fraction of this number of Christian missionaries in the world today, one is impressed with the zealous response that will come out of Israel in the form of faith in Jesus Christ as its Messiah. "The gospel of the Kingdom" will be preached with great zeal by them to the world.

Bringing Forth Gentile Saints

God's second purpose for the period of judgments known as the Tribulation, the last three and one-half years which is called the Great Tribulation, is to save, through their belief in Jesus, a great host of Gentile (non-Jewish) people, who will be a part of His family for eternity.

Again, Dave Breese explains:

> The Tribulation will also be a time of massive conversion of Gentile multitudes. The Revelation says, after this I beheld, and, lo, a great multitude, which no man could number, of all nations, and kindreds, and people, and tongues, stood before the throne, and before the Lamb, clothed with white robes, and palms in their hands (Rev. 7:9). So remarkable is this sight that one of the elders around God's throne asked who these people are. The answer from the Word of God is: "These are they who came out of the great tribulation, and have washed their robes, and made them white in the blood of the Lamb" (Rev. 7:14).

> Amazing spiritual results occur when the world comes to the end of itself, realizing that nothing on earth is of any value. It then turns in great numbers to faith in Christ as Messiah, bringing in a time of evangelism that will be one of the largest and most effective in the history of the world. The anguish of the Tribulation produces a most salutary result. But a fearful time it will be! (Breese, p. 297).

Overview of Tribulation Terrors

It is wonderful to consider that we who are Christians will be in Heaven with our Lord Jesus while all the prophesied horrors of the seven years of Tribulation are unfolding on earth. The Rapture is mockingly called "pie in the sky—in the sweet by and by," and "wishful escapism," by those who don't believe in a Rapture, or who believe Christians must prove how brave and strong we are by standing up to Antichrist in going through what Jesus called the worst time that has ever been or will ever be on this planet.

There are some things that Jesus indicated are well worth escaping. We will look more in-depth at the most horrendous of the Judgments in the next lesson. For now, this might be a good place to put the things scheduled following the Rapture, according to prophecy, in a nutshell for quick review.

Following the Rapture of Christ's saints (all born-again believers who are alive at the time it occurs), prophesied things will start popping quickly.

- Total chaos will rule for a time.
- Governments will get control through sometimes-harsh methods.
- One world government will come together.
- A one-world church will form.
- A world leader from Europe will step to the forefront and take charge of the peace process.
- Israeli government and Israel's enemies will sign an agreement of peace that ensures peace and safety.
- Peace will not last, as a coalition of nations, led by Russia, will invade the Middle East.
- God, Himself, will destroy all but one-sixth of the invader forces.
- Much of the world will be hit by the deadly effects of the invasion. This will possibly include chemical, biological and nuclear aftereffects.
- The world leader will solidify his power following the Russian-led coalition's destruction.
- Two Old-Testament-type prophets will come on the world scene and preach about Christ, while condemning the world's evil.
- Meanwhile, God will put His protection upon 144,000 Jews who have converted to Christianity so that they can begin to preach God's saving message to the people of the Tribulation.
- At the same time, God will allow strong delusion to come over all who heard the gospel before the Rapture, but, fully understanding the offer of salvation, refused to accept Christ. These will believe Antichrist's and Satan's lies.
- Antichrist, after months of trying, will finally murder the two Old-Testament-type prophets. But they will come back to life and be taken into Heaven while the world watches.
- Antichrist will receive a supposedly deadly head wound.
- He will appear to resurrect from the dead, being now possessed by Satan.

- Antichrist will stand in the Temple on Mount Moriah in Jerusalem. He will claim to be God, and demand worship.
- The false prophet will direct all worship to Antichrist, and will erect an image of him.
- Antichrist's regime will institute a computer mark and numbers system. It will be both to control the world's populations and to cause all to worship Antichrist, whose number in all of this is 666.
- Those who refuse to accept Antichrist's mark will be murdered. Beheading will apparently be the regime's chosen method of offing these "traitors."
- Antichrist will begin a systematic genocide against the Jewish race that will make Hitler's holocaust look mild by comparison.
- He and the false prophet will also have all the new believers they can find, rounded up, tortured, then murdered.
- While Antichrist hunts down and murders people by the millions, God's judgments will begin to fall directly on the rebellious people of planet Earth.
- Millions upon millions will die while God's wrath pours out in a series of three types of judgments, each consisting of seven specific judgments, for a total of 21 judgments.
- When all is said and done, more than one-half, possibly as much as two-thirds, of all human life on Earth will die of the plagues.
- God will prepare, and the Jewish remnant will flee to, a hiding place, probably Petra, the ancient city carved in the rose red-colored rocks of the Jordanian wilderness.
- Antichrist and his forces, led by Satan, will pursue the Jewish people and try to murder them, but the pursuing forces will be swallowed up by the Earth.
- While the Jewish and many of the Gentile people still alive remain safely protected, God's wrath will fall in greater force.
- The sun will go partly dark, while at the same time heating up to seven times hotter than normal.

- A great object will fall into the ocean from space. Its impact will kill life in the sea, and most likely will destroy coastal areas with tidal waves.
- Another asteroid or other mass from space will strike Earth and will poison much of the planet's fresh water sources.
- Great, unprecedented earthquakes will happen simultaneously all over the Earth.
- People will be so frightened they will have heart attacks, just from the things they see are yet to come.
- A supernatural plague of huge insect-like creatures will be released from the abyss, and they will sting all who have the mark of the beast. Men and women will try to commit suicide because of their great pain from the stings and bites of these demonic creatures.
- God will then move in the minds of all military forces on Earth to gather in the valley of Jezreel, the plains of Esdraelon, near the ancient city of Megiddo. This is Armageddon.
- The "Kings of the East," a huge army out of the Orient numbering more than 200 million troops, will invade to make war with Antichrist's and the other world's forces.
- Jesus said of this time, that if He didn't come back, everyone and everything would die because of the fighting about to take place.
- Jesus will return with the armies of Heaven. His armies consist of the mighty angels and His saints, which were raptured at least seven years earlier.
- Antichrist's armies and all others will try to prevent Christ's return.
- Jesus will simply speak, and all armies on Earth will be rendered helpless, most killed.

Scary stuff, huh? But it will all happen. You have God's Word on that. A bunch of good reasons to be "Rapture ready," and to be found worthy to stand before Jesus, don't you think?

Again, Dave Breese informs us about the coming time of Tribulation—a time the Lord says will be unlike any other in terms of catastrophes experienced by people of planet Earth.

God's Wrath Poured Forth

"The Tribulation is the time of the outpouring of the wrath of God upon a wicked world. In the account of the horsemen of the Apocalypse, when the fourth horseman rides forth, the Scripture says, power was given unto them over the fourth part of earth to kill with sword, and with hunger, and with death, and with the beasts of the earth (Rev. 6:8). In the beginning days of the Revelation, therefore, approximately 25 percent of the world is killed in the opening wars pestilence's of days. Very quickly, the Scripture says, 'And thus I saw the horses in the vision, and them that sat on them, having breastplates of fire, and of jacinth, and brimstone: and the heads of the horses were as the heads of lions; and out of their mouths issued fire and smoke and brimstone. By these three was the third part of men killed, by the fire, and by the smoke, and by the brimstone, which issued out of their mouths' (Rev. 9:17-18).

A third part of men killed! This already mounts up to one half of the world's population, and beyond this point in the Revelation many other natural catastrophes take place. As the Tribulation unfolds, there are mighty earthquakes, occasions of scorching heat, the advent of the Antichrist, world occult religious organizations, and finally, the Battle of Armageddon, which will be fatal to scores of millions of soldiers. This time of natural catastrophe combined with divine judgment will bring awesome carnage across the face of the earth" (Breese, p. 297-298).

Earth's Darkest Hours Approach

Just a quick look around us today lets us know that stage setting for the things prophesied to take place during the Tribulation is upon us. The darkest hours of human history loom not too far in the distance.

Words of Comfort

What tremendous power there is in the knowledge that we who name the name of Christ during this Pre-Tribulation age will not have to endure the things that are surely coming to a world in rebellion against our Mighty God. Again, we know we won't have to face God's anger and judgment for sin, based upon—for one example—the prophetic words of Paul to us through the Thessalonian Christians nearly 2 millennia ago. "For God hath not appointed us to wrath, but to obtain salvation by our Lord Jesus Christ, Who died for us, that, whether we wake or sleep, we should live together with him. Wherefore comfort yourselves together, and edify one another, even as also ye do" (1 Thess. 5:9-11).

Let us indeed comfort ourselves with these words. Let us, at the same time, do all within our power—and that power, through Jesus, is considerable—to reach the lost before it's too late for them to avoid the horrors coming upon the earth.

For Additional Study

1. When did God's wrath first fall upon earth?

2. When will God's wrath next fall, according to Bible prophecy?

3. How many judgments will fall during the Tribulation?

4. Will there be peace between Israel and her enemies before Christ's return?

5. What causes God's wrath to again fall upon earth-dwellers?

6. What Scriptures prophesy Antichrist, and the treaty of false peace?

7. What is the twofold purpose of God's judgment during the Tribulation?

8. List as many prophesied events as you can that will happen following the Rapture.

9. Approximately people will die during the Tribulation?

Hell on Earth

KEY PROPHECY POWER TRUTH

"Alas! for that day is great, so that none is like it: it is even the time of Jacob's trouble."

Jeremiah 30:7

The Raptured saints most likely will have received rewards earned in this life by the time the Tribulation is full-blown. We must remember, however, that God is outside of the time he has created for mankind. He is timeless, and we can't really know how heavenly activity corresponds to earthly time. It seems, however, that the prophetic Word indicates the Bema rewards judgment is completed by the time the scrolls are unsealed by Jesus Christ, the Lamb of God.

This is so because the 24 elders—most likely representing the 12 patriarchs of the Old Testament, and the 12 apostles, representing the New Testament—are seated in the throne room of God, witnessing the events as Jesus is asked to unseal the seven-sealed scroll of Judgment. (Read Revelation, chapters 4 through 6.)

Christians, with their rewards, have probably been assigned duties, possibly even duties that include interacting in some way with activities involving the Tribulation. This is speculation, but nonetheless is possible, because Heaven will be a realm of tremendously dynamic activity, not a place where we all play harps and sit around looking pious in white robes.

The placement of that great event known as the Marriage Supper of the Lamb must also be considered in thinking on things going on at the same time the horrors of the Tribulation are unfolding.

The catastrophic events prophesied by Jesus and the prophets will slam into planet Earth with increasing violence and rapidity. Billions will die, and, if Jesus didn't descend from Heaven to personally put an end to the carnage, He said there would be no one left alive.

We've seen before that the Apostle Paul often used sports terms to teach principles of godly living. We are told we wrestle against evil, we run in the race of life, we must not beat the air, as a boxer does when shadow boxing.

Paul's teaching style, using sports analogies, fits very well, while we consider the final years, months, days, and hours of human history, just before Jesus returns in His Second Coming. We will look at the seven years of Tribulation as the great climax in the battle of good versus evil. It will be a fight to determine who is the real Champion for eternity.

Although it won't be much of a fight, from the standpoint of competition, it will be the bloodiest of all conflicts ever!

The Seal Judgments

God calls upon His Son, Jesus, the Lamb of God, to open the seals that will unleash righteous judgment upon a world that has totally rejected the Father's call to salvation. With Jesus releasing the judgments of God from the very first scroll, we know that it's God's wrath from the very beginning of the seven-year Tribulation period. The championship battle to prove who is and is not the champion for eternity begins.

The four horsemen of the Apocalypse will ride forth upon command by Jesus, as He unrolls each of the first four sealed scrolls. These will be the opening rounds of this bloody battle.

Round One: White Horse of False Peace

The first rider, on the white horse, is Antichrist, who will come offering peace (Rev. 6:2). As we've already discussed, he is really a deceiver and a conqueror, however. He will promise prosperity, and freedom to do whatever feels good. But, the jubilation over the fact that the Christians are gone, thus can't preach at earth-dwellers, won't last long. Antichrist's true colors will begin to show. They will be blood-red! The peace he offers will destroy millions (read Daniel 8:25)

Round Two: Red Horse of War
The second rider, on a red horse, is the rider of war (Rev. 6:4). The false peace Antichrist promised will be broken, and millions will die from unprecedented wars. All the wars will be a prelude to the ultimate war, Armageddon!

Round Three: Black Horse of Famine
The third rider, on a black horse, is famine (Rev. 6:5). Millions upon millions will die of starvation and other results of the all-out war making ushered in by the rider on the red horse.

We have only to consider the great world wars of the last century, and all the other wars, to know that hunger and disease inevitably follow the carnage of all-out war. Considering that some of the future wars will include nuclear, biological, and chemical weaponry, the probability of great hunger and disease multiply many times.

Round Four: Pale Horse of Death
The fourth rider, on a pale horse, has a partner riding close behind. The front rider is death (Rev. 6:8). Sheol, the abode of the dead non-believers, will follow. These riders will account for the death of one-fourth of the world's population. The disease and famine will continue to mount.

Round Five: Martyrs
When Jesus opens the fifth seal, the saints of the Tribulation era who have been martyred for Christ will be seen in their white robes of salvation before God's throne (Rev. 6:9-11).

Many prophetic scholars believe that the Tribulation era will produce the greatest soul-harvest ever. Many believe the numbers saved during this time will far surpass the number of people saved during the Church Age.

Round Six: Earth-Shaking Events

As the sixth seal is opened, there will be a great earthquake, the sun will darken, and the moon will turn red (Rev. 6:12-14). These events will so frighten the leaders of Earth that they will beg the rocks and caves in which they are hiding to fall on them, and conceal them from the furious God of Heaven. No wonder the prophetic Scripture tells us that men's hearts will fail them for fear of the things they see coming upon the earth.

And yet earth-dwellers will still not repent, but will actually curse God!

Round Seven: Getting a Breather

Unlike human athletes, God needs no breaks to catch His breath. But, He seems to take a breather in anticipation of the next catastrophic set of judgments with the opening of the seventh seal: a thirty-minute period of silence in Heaven (Rev. 8:1, 2). Following that quiet time, seven angels standing before God will be given the seven trumpets.

Prophetic Pattern

Most prophecy scholars see this is a pattern God always follows in rendering His judgments, or between taking action in a series. For example, in Genesis, He takes the seventh day off from all the work He had done in the creation. He, therefore, takes a short time out between the sixth and seventh seals. But the pause doesn't change the minds and hearts of the evil ones who oppose him.

The Trumpet Judgments

God then prepares to step up the pace of judgment against the foolish Earth dwellers as the trumpet judgments begin.

Round Eight (First Trumpet): Hail, Fire and Blood

After the angel sounds the first trumpet, hail and fire mixed with blood will fall from Heaven. The fire will cause all green grass and a third of the Earth's trees to burn up (Rev. 8:6, 7). Certainly, it will already appear to be the end of the world as we know it. God will fire off a stunning blow to those who will not repent of their sin against Him. But this will be just the beginning of His body blows to the planet.

Round Nine (Second Trumpet): Burning Mountain

Something that appeared to John to look like a burning mountain will be cast into the sea. A third of the sea will turn to blood, a third of all sea life will die, and a third of the ships at sea will be destroyed (Rev. 8:8, 9).

This will be a stupendous blow to a planet already reeling because of God's judgments. Any time God's Word uses phrases like "as it were" (Rev. 8:8), it is a symbolic description to show something that is figurative. In other words, this will not be a literal mountain, but it will be "like" a mountain in size. It really will be a big rock that's on fire, and it sounds much like the asteroids, meteors, and other rocks from space that pose danger to our planet. This prophecy appears to forewarn that something like that will slam into one of Earth's oceans.

This event will be catastrophic to Earth's environment, because the Bible says that the sea will become like blood, thick and slimy—apparently like blood plasma. A third of sea life will die and a third of all ships will be destroyed by the tremendous tidal waves.

Round Ten (Third Trumpet): Star Called Wormwood

A heavenly object of some sort called "Wormwood" will cause another great blow to Earth's water supplies as it

---

Modern Incident Involving "Wormwood"

The word "wormwood" is quite interesting. As has been noted by many who write on prophetic matters, the word "wormwood" in the Ukrainian language is "Chernobyl." Sound familiar? This is the town in the Ukraine infamous for the worst nuclear power plant disaster to date. The object falling from space, as described in this judgment, might well be nuclear in nature, perhaps a nuclear-tipped missile.

crashes into the planet. This time the fresh waters will be poisoned, and people who drink from the affected waters will die (Rev. 8:10, 11).

Round Eleven (Fourth Trumpet): Darkness

The Earth's inhabitants will next receive a black eye, so to speak, so that their vision will be severely affected. The sun will darken by one-third, so naturally the moon, a reflective body, will also have its light diminished by one-third. The stars also will be supernaturally darkened (Rev. 8:12).

God seems to step back and size up His opponent before moving in to punish the rebels of Earth even more. The ringside announcer—an angel—will announce that the next judgments will be even worse than the first (Rev. 8:13).

Round Twelve (Fifth Trumpet): Plague of Locusts

God apparently allows an angelic being to open the abyss, or "bottomless pit," releasing the weirdest, most fearsome creatures ever seen on Earth (Rev. 9:1-5). They are described as being like scorpions whose stings hurt people for five months. Many scholars of prophecy are convinced the angelic being is Satan, who will fall to Earth when he is cast out of Heaven during the Tribulation, and that the creatures are a horde of demons.

Round Thirteen (Sixth Trumpet):
Army of Evil Horsemen

God will order the unbinding of demonic beings, whose habitation is somewhere beneath the Euphrates River (Rev. 9:15-21). These are angels who followed Lucifer in his original rebellion against the Lord. They apparently will enter into and possess the 200 million troops that come from the Orient, which is east of the Euphrates. These tremendous numbers are referred to as "the kings of the East" in Revelation 16:12.

The might of these forces will be awesome. They will inflict horrific damage on all in their path. Another one-third of the people left on the Earth will die because of their war making. Still, rebellious people will not repent and bow before God.

Round Fourteen (Seventh Trumpet): Heralding the Bowl Judgments

Again, God will pause in His assault on His evil opponents. He will stop between the sixth and seventh trumpet judgments to tell all the things that will take place between the blowing of the sixth trumpet and the beginning of the vial, or bowl, judgments. These awesome prophetic events include the two witnesses' time on the Tribulation scene; the 144,000 sealed super-evangelists; the whole story of Satan's hatred for Jesus and the Jewish race, and the rise and fall of Antichrist.

Round Fifteen (Bowl One): Sores

The next assault will begin with the pouring out of the first of the seven deadly bowls of the pure wrath of the living God. Unbelievably horrible sores will infect all who have rejected God.

Round Sixteen (Bowl Two): Bloody Sea

Before they switched to 12 rounders as maximum, the 15th round in a world championship fight was the last one. In this battle of the ages, the fight will be just getting heated up. And, it will be one-sided. Judgments from God are so frightful, the prophet John must have had to totally depend upon the Lord for the words to describe them: "And the second angel poured out his vial upon the sea; and it became as the blood of a dead man: and every living soul died in the sea" (Rev. 16:3).

God's Word, through John, doesn't even attempt to describe what will be poured into the sea. But it will kill every living thing, whatever it is. The water will become like a dead man's blood. Imagine! Water with the viscosity, and apparently, the stench and grotesqueness of coagulating blood.

Round Seventeen (Bowl Three): Bloody Rivers

The third angel will pour out his bowl into the fresh waters, and they will turn to blood (Rev. 16:4). The judgments are indeed fearsome, but God is totally righteous in inflicting them upon the inhabitants of Earth who have rejected Him. We hear the voices from God's corner urging him onward, as the fight continues: "Thou art righteous, O Lord, which art, and wast, and shalt be, because thou hast judged thus. For they have shed the blood of saints and prophets, and thou hast given them blood to drink; for they are worthy" (Rev. 16:5, 6).

Round Eighteen (Bowl Four): Scorching Heat

God will pound the Earth with heavier and heavier blows. As the fourth angel pours out his bowl on the sun, it apparently goes into partial nova. That is, it will shrink and grow darker. Yet at the same time, it will get much hotter. Men cannot escape the scorching, killing heat. Rather than beg for forgiveness, they will curse God's holy name! (Rev. 16:8, 9).

Round Nineteen (Bowl Five): Darkness and Pain

God pours His judgments directly upon the most rebellious of the rebels. Apparently, ultraviolet rays from the dying sun will laser through Earth's unprotected atmosphere and cause skin eruptions on those not sealed with God's protection. They will gnaw their tongues in agony, but when they do manage to speak intelligible words, they will speak curses against the Lord (Rev. 16:10, 11).

Round Twenty (Bowl Six): Euphrates Dries Up

Next, God will allow total demonic activity to take place upon Earth. The vilest demonic spirits apparently will be unleashed in the area of the Euphrates River. These spirits will enter into the military forces of the world, and tremendous death and destruction from the great campaign called Armageddon (for it is a war campaign, not just a single, final battle) will intensify by the minute (Rev. 16:12-14).

The hordes from the Orient called "the kings of the east" will be allowed easy access to the Middle East because the Euphrates River, a natural barrier to land forces, is dried up.

Round Twenty-One (Bowl Seven):
Greatest of all Earthquakes and
Hundred-Pound Hailstones

The final tremendous blow from God's great right hand of judgment—following His weighty words, "It is done," will

---

Pause for the Big Finish

Before the seventh bowl will be poured out, Almighty God pauses to say something about those who are His own: "Behold, I come as a thief. Blessed is he that watcheth, and keepeth his garments, lest he walk naked, and they see his shame. And he gathered them together into a place called in the Hebrew tongue Armageddon. And the seventh angel poured out his vial into the air; and there came a great voice out of the temple of heaven, from the throne, saying, It is done!" (Rev. 16:15-17).

He seems to cover all from the Church Age through the Tribulation who are Christians. His words for saints seem to commend them for watching for Christ's any-moment return. He says He will come unannounced and suddenly upon an unsuspecting world. He will come "as a thief" because it will be an unanticipated, unwelcome break-in upon the world of rebels who do not know or want Him.

His own, however, should be watching for Him. They shouldn't be surprised by an unwelcome break-in upon their lives. They should never be comfortable with living like the rest of the world.

He gives blessings to the Tribulation saints for keeping their robes of righteousness by being faithful to Him. They did so in the face of the rebels who wanted to see them disrobe, that is, to deny Christ.

---

come in the form of a devastating earthquake and giant hailstones that flatten every city on the planet. Jerusalem will split into three parts. Entire islands will disappear under the titanic blow (Rev. 16:18-20). What could stand under the pounding of hailstones that weigh more than 100 pounds each? The rebels are literally pounded into submission in this final round of judgments. The Babylonian system of godless humanism, commercialism and religion will come to an end (Revelation, chapters 17 and 18).

This will be the fulfillment of the dream-vision Daniel the prophet interpreted for Nebuchadnezzar, king of Babylon. Jesus, symbolically the stone from Heaven, will strike the metallic man-image on the feet and 10 toes, and all of the Babylonian, humanistic governmental system of history will crumble and fall. The debris will be blown away by the winds of Eternity. (Read Daniel, chapter 2.)

***

It really isn't much of a fight, is it? To put it in juvenile fight language: "There wasn't really but two punches thrown." God hits His enemies, and His enemies hit the ground.

Powerful Promise

God, even through dispensing judgment, does so in steps. He does so through His supreme love. He gives everyone a chance to repent—to turn to Him.

Each of us who name the name of Christ should appropriate the power that is in the promise of God that we won't face His Wrath. That understanding should give each Christian strength to live life to the fullest, knowing that ours is a God of might, and of Truth!

What Will Happen to Those Who Take the Mark

Being left behind when the rapture occurs will be no blessing. Besides being cast into the lake of fire (Revelation 14:9, 10), here is just a partial list of the terrible things those who take the mark of the beast will face if they are lucky enough to live very long:

1. Violent wars (Rev. 6:3, 4; 9:15-18).
2. Economic collapse, hunger and starvation (Rev. 6:5, 6).
3. Famine, pestilence and wild animals (Rev. 6:7, 8).
4. Earthquakes, extreme darkness and perhaps nuclear bombs and missiles (Rev. 6:12).
5. Hail and fire that burns one-third of the trees and grass on earth (Rev. 8:7).
6. One-third of the sea turning to blood (Rev. 8:8, 9).
7. One-third of the fresh water being polluted (Rev. 8:10,11).
8. One-third of the sun, moon and stars being darkened (Rev. 8:12).
9. Demon-possessed locusts with the sting of scorpions (Rev. 9:3-5).
10. Painful sores (Rev. 16:2).
11. Worldwide pollution of the seas (Rev. 16:2).
12. Worldwide pollution of fresh water (Rev. 16:4).
13. Scorching fire from the sun (Rev. 16:8).
14. Total darkness with extreme agony on earth (Rev. 16:10).

(Daymond Duck's chapter, "Forewarning the Final Fuhrer," in William T. James' book, *Piercing the Future: Prophecy and the New Millennium* (Benton, AR: Nelson Walker Publishers, 2000) p. 321-322.

For Additional Study

1 Why can't we know the exact time Bema judgments are finished in relation to the Tribulation on earth?

2. Why is it likely that the Bema judgment is over by the time Christ unseals the first of the 7 scrolls of Revelation chapter 6?

3. Who is called upon to unleash God's judgments during the Tribulation?

4. From what point in the seals unsealing does God's wrath begin to fall on the earth?

5. Name the colors of the horses of the 4 horsemen of Revelation, chapter 6.

6. Give the horsemen in order, and what each represents as judgments.

7. How many deaths will these riders cause upon earth?

8. How will rebellious earth-dwellers react to the increasingly intense judgments from God?

9. What is the final judgment sent upon the rebels of earth?

Christ's Return, Reign, and Restoration

KEY PROPHECY POWER TRUTH

"And I saw heaven opened, and behold a white horse; and he that sat upon him was called Faithful and True, and in righteousness he doth judge and make war."

Revelation 19:11

Some within the numbers of those who study Bible prophecy are strongly at odds with the Pre-Tribulation view of the Rapture. Remember, the Pre-Trib view proclaims that Jesus will return for His saints before the seven years of Tribulation, also known as "Daniel's Seventieth Week."

Those against the Pre-Trib view—sometimes with considerable anger in their opposition—declare that Christians must go through the Tribulation in order to wash their robes white. In other words, we who are Christians must, the anti-Pre-Tribbers proclaim, endure until the end, in order to prove ourselves worthy to then be raptured at the mid-point, or at the end of the Tribulation.

No Wrath for Christians!

But, again, the Apostle Paul, under divine direction of the Holy Spirit, tells us: "For God hath not appointed us to wrath, but to obtain salvation by our Lord Jesus Christ, Who died for us, that, whether we wake or sleep, we should live together with him" (1 Thess. 5:9, 10).

As we have seen previously, Paul, speaking to Church Age saints, says further: "Wherefore comfort yourselves together, and edify one another, even as also ye do" (1 Thess. 5:11).

Last-Days Mockers Miss God's Truth About Return

Those who mock the Pre-Trib Rapture of Christ's saints see not two phases to Christ's Second Coming (1- the Rapture; 2- His return to earth), but one only. They believe the saints of Jesus Christ, will win the many conflicts for God during that terrible Tribulation time. But God's Word says of Antichrist: "And it was given unto him to make war with the saints, and to overcome them: and power was given him over all kindreds, and tongues, and nations" (Rev.13:7). So, the Lord's churches will not prevail over Antichrist during the Tribulation. Neither will Antichrist prevail over the churches of Jesus Christ. Because these churches won't be on Earth during that era of horrors.

Church Will Prevail Upon the Rock!

Another reason we know that Antichrist can't overcome the Lord's churches is that God's Word contradicts the thought that a church must go through the time when Antichrist rules on earth. The Scripture that proves this is: "And I say also unto thee, That thou art Peter, and upon this rock I will build my church; and the gates of hell shall not prevail against it" (Matt.16:18).

So during the Tribulation, Satan's forces will overcome the saints. During the time of building Christ's churches, Satan's forces will not be able to prevail. God's Word speaks of two separate groups of saints: 1) the Church Age saints, and 2) the Tribulation era saints.

Looking for Christ, not Antichrist

Beyond this proof, however, is God's Word to all Christians. He tells us nowhere in the Bible to look for Tribulation, or for suffering that is greater than any people have ever suffered, or will ever suffer following that terrible time. God's Word doesn't warn saints to be watching for Antichrist. The prophetic Word of God tells us, again through Paul's words to the saints: "Looking for that blessed hope, and the glorious appearing of the great God and our Saviour Jesus Christ" (Titus 2:13).

We are not to fear a great time of suffering; we are to comfort one another with the knowledge Christ will keep us out of that time of Tribulation (Rev. 3:10).

Look Up!

Christians living during these days are told additionally: "When these things [signals of the Tribulation] begin to come to pass, then look up, and lift up your heads; for your redemption draweth nigh" (Luke 21:28).

Christians Have Round-trip Ticket!

We who are Christians during this present dispensation will have been Raptured to Heaven at least seven-years earlier than the time of Christ's return at the Second Advent. We will return with the Lord Jesus at the moment He bursts through the clouds of glory to put an end to the armies who have gathered to slaughter each other, and to oppose Him.

Jesus, the King of all kings and Lord of all lords, will then rule and reign over this judgment—torn planet, and will restore it to like it was at the time of the Garden of Eden.

In His Majesty's Supernatural Service!

You and I will serve Him in ways we can't even begin to imagine from this side of our meeting Him face to face. What a soul-empowering truth!

Let us do our best to understand what that era will be like. We will begin by looking at Armageddon, and will examine prophesied things that go through the end of the Millennium (Christ's 1000-year reign on earth).

The first thing to look at is the majestic coming again of Christ. "And I saw heaven opened, and behold a white horse; and he that sat upon him was called Faithful and True, and in righteousness he doth judge and make war. His eyes were as a flame of fire, and on his head were many crowns; and he had a name written, that no man knew, but he himself. And he was clothed with a vesture dipped in blood: and his name is called The Word of God. And the armies which were in heaven followed him upon white horses, clothed in fine linen, white and clean. And out of his mouth goeth a sharp sword, that with it he should smite the nations: and he shall rule them with a rod of iron: and he treadeth the winepress of the fierceness and wrath of Almighty God" (Rev. 19:11-15).

Armageddon

No other word so strikes fear when thinking about troubles in the Middle East than does the word "Armageddon." Any time conflict in that geographical area bubbles to the surface in a major way, all the world's focus zeros in on the region. Immediately, news media and many people within and without Christianity seek out biblical prophecy scholars, writers, broadcasters, and clergy in general to ask: "Might this be the beginning of Armageddon?"

It's amazing. The worry and frenzy to know about Armageddon quickly dies, when it becomes evident that the world will wag on as usual. But, for those few fearful hours, or days, everyone's attention is on the prophesied event known as Armageddon. The fear is well-founded, for the prophecy indicates it will be a fearsome time like none other.

We've looked at the judgments of God that get progressively worse while the seven years of Tribulation continue toward Christ's return. Armageddon is fought while many of those horrific Judgments are occurring.

War Campaign Called Armageddon

Armageddon is thought of as a battle. We hear most often the term *the Battle of Armageddon.* But it is actually a campaign of many battles. It will rage throughout much of the time of Tribulation. The war-making will come to a climax at Megiddo, also called in the Hebrew language Armageddon. Thus, it is called the battle of Armageddon. Actually, Armageddon doesn't get the chance to fully play out on the Plains of Esdraelon, in the Valley of Jezreel, near the ancient mound-city called Megiddo. Jesus will put an end to the war, while all the armies of the world gather there for man's final conflict.

Christ's Merciful Intervention

Jesus' devastating intervention will be not only an act of vengeance upon those who will not repent, it will be a great act of God's mercy. Jesus, Himself, commented on His putting a stop to man's insane warmaking. He said: "And except that the Lord had shortened those days, no flesh should be saved: but for the elect's sake, whom he hath chosen, he hath shortened the days" (Mark 13:20).

The Lord Jesus will stop Armageddon. He will do so in order to prevent His elect—Tribulation saints scattered throughout the world—from being killed by the horrendous weaponry that will no doubt be available to the leaders of the armies gathered in that great triangular valley just north of Israel.

Saints Return to Earth

The raptured saints will ride with Jesus, while He descends from Heaven to put an end to all war caused by the sins of mankind. The prophet, Jude, wrote: "And Enoch also, the seventh from Adam, prophesied of these, saying, Behold, the Lord cometh with ten thousands of his saints, To execute judgment upon all, and to convince all that are ungodly among them of all their ungodly deeds which they have ungodly committed, and of all their hard speeches which ungodly sinners have spoken against him" (Jude 14, 15).

Again, Christ's elect who must be rescued by the Lord's intervention are the Tribulation saints (those who have been saved during that seven-year period). The saints of the Church Age were raptured at least seven years prior to Armageddon. They return with the King of kings to stop the intentions of the armies of the world to engage in the most horrific battle of human history.

Peace, Be Still . . .

Leaders of the forces who meet at Armageddon to battle each other will turn to see the brightness that has broken through the darkness that has overcast Earth's skies because of the judgments of God. Antichrist, supreme leader of much of the forces west of the Euphrates River, will recognize the invading force from Heaven. Perhaps the leaders from the 200-million-man army from the Orient that has crossed the dried-up Euphrates from the east will also know what the brilliantly shining heavenly intrusion is all about. All earthly forces will then turn to concentrate their fire at the descending heavenly army, led by Jesus Christ.

While the sea of humanity on the planet's surface viciously roars in an attempt to prevent the heavenly intervention, those warring forces will turn from battling with each other to curse God and all His righteousness. Then Jesus Christ, mounted upon a stunningly white steed, will speak words sharper than a two-edged sword.

Master To Calm Storm

I am convinced they will be the same words Jesus of Nazareth spoke to that raging Sea of Galilee nearly two millennia ago. (Read Mark 4:36-41.) They are the same words He speaks today to everyone who turns to Him, acknowledging that there is nothing and no one but Christ who can save them. He speaks those words to all who accept Him and trust Him to save them from their sins and to make them born-again children of God.

Just as His words instantaneously calmed that violent sea, thus saving the men in the little boat, Jesus' words will instantly end the warfare and rebellion at Armageddon. Christ's words to the individual's troubled heart likewise bring tranquility and joy to the soul. A Person is never the same when Jesus speaks those life-changing words. "Peace, be still" (Mark 4:39).

Bloody Peace

When Jesus speaks the words, "Peace, be still" at Armageddon, His command will be against all the vileness that has been building in humanistic rebellion over the thousands of years since God last judged in such a mighty way. All people died in the Flood except Noah and seven others. Christ's words at Armageddon will apparently cause most if not all of the soldiers of the armies of the world gathered there to literally burst open, so powerful will be His command. The plains of Armageddon will flow with a flood of blood! The Scripture says of this event: "And the winepress was trodden without the city, and blood came out of the winepress, even unto the horse bridles, by the space of a thousand and six hundred furlongs" (Rev. 14:20).

The point is, when Jesus speaks, His words are sharper and more powerful than a two-edged sword, the Scripture says. When Christ speaks, all opposition by earth's armies will instantly cease and desist. All will lie horribly bloody— but peaceful—upon the vast killing field called Armageddon.

Jesus on the Throne!

Jesus, following His stunning victory over the enemies of God, will proceed to get the people of Israel who have, during the Tribulation, come to believe in Him. He will rescue them from the place God has hidden them. This hiding of believing Israel (all Jewish people who have accepted that Jesus was, and is their Messiah) is revealed in the following Scriptures: "And when the dragon saw that he was cast unto the earth, he persecuted the woman which brought forth the man child. And to the woman were given two wings of a great eagle, that she might fly into the wilderness, into her place, where she is nourished for a time, and times, and half a time, from the face of the serpent. And the serpent cast out of his mouth water as a flood after the woman, that he might cause her to be carried away of the flood. And the earth helped the woman, and the earth opened her mouth, and swallowed up the flood which the dragon cast out of his mouth. And the dragon was wroth with the woman, and went to make war with the remnant of her seed, which keep the commandments of God, and have the testimony of Jesus Christ" (Rev. 12:13-17).

The Hiding Place

Satan's Antichrist forces will try to completely wipe the Jewish race from the face of the Earth. But, God will intervene with great supernatural catastrophe, and prevent the Antichrist from finding the Jews. God will have hidden them somewhere.

Many prophetic scholars believe the hiding place will be in the Jordanian desert, in the "rose-red city" called Petra. Jesus will retrieve these believing Jews from their hiding place, and will use this remnant of the Jewish race to be His nation of Israel during His 1000-year rule on earth.

Israel Saved

The Bible says one-third of Jews alive during the Tribulation will recognize their Messiah, Jesus Christ, at the moment He returns in the Second Coming. It will be a real eye-opener for them. "And I will pour upon the house of David, and upon the inhabitants of Jerusalem, the spirit of grace and of supplications: and they shall look upon me whom they have pierced, and they shall mourn for him, as one mourneth for his only son, and shall be in bitterness for him, as one that is in bitterness for his firstborn" (Zech. 12:10).

Jesus will then move, with His saints and with His chosen people (all of saved Israel), to Jerusalem. He will set up His throne upon a topographically changed Mt. Moriah in the Millennial Temple He will build.

Antichrist and False Prophet Judgment

The Lord Jesus will judge Antichrist and the False Prophet, who have persecuted Tribulation saints, and, particularly, the Jewish race (Israel). We learn of these two beasts as follows: "And the beast was taken, and with him the false prophet that wrought miracles before him, with which he deceived them that had received the mark of the beast, and them that worshipped his image. These both were cast alive into a lake of fire burning with brimstone" (Rev. 19:20).

These two will be the first to be cast into hell. They will have it to themselves until 1000 years later, after the White Throne Judgment, which will be looked at in the next lesson.

Satan's Confinement

The Devil will next be grabbed and confined for 1000 years: "And I saw an angel come down from heaven, having the key of the bottomless pit and a great chain in his hand. And he laid hold on the dragon, that old serpent, which is the Devil, and Satan, and bound him a thousand years, And cast him into the bottomless pit, and shut him up, and set a seal upon him, that he should deceive the nations no more, till the thousand years should be fulfilled: and after that he must be loosed a little season" (Rev. 20:1-3).

Sheep and Goat Judgments

Christ will judge the nations. Their fate will hang upon how they treated His chosen people, the Jews. The "goat" nations will stand on Christ's left while He judges, while the "sheep" nations will stand on His right. All in the "goat" nations will be cast into everlasting darkness. They are lost for eternity. These nations consist of individually lost souls, each of whom will, apparently, be placed in nations that have persecuted Jews, and, most likely, Tribulation saints as well. The nations so judged will no longer be part of the nations of earth. (Read Matthew 25:32-46 to learn exactly what the prophetic Word of God has to say about that great future judgment.)

It is logical to presume that the saved people who have lived in the "goat" or lost nations will be put into the "sheep" nations, which will be allowed into the millennial kingdom. Likewise, the unsaved people who have lived in the "sheep" nations will go into the "goat" nations to meet their eternal fate in outer darkness.

Saints of the Tribulation who make it through the seven years alive, will, individually, go into the nations that have treated Israel kindly. However, it must be recognized that the children who will be born during the Millennium will have to make the same decision their parents made to accept or reject Christ for salvation. Millions will not do so, and will be as rebellious as were the rebels before this time of Christ's glorious reign on earth for 1000 years. These unsaved will join Satan in the final rebellion when he is released from the bottomless pit for a brief time. All will be destroyed, and will spend eternity in the lake of fire apart from God.

Millions of others who are the children of the saints that go into the Millennium will accept Christ, and will, ultimately, live eternally with God. These offspring of the Tribulation saints who go into the Millennium will be the people who will continue to repopulate the earth for 1000 years. All of these individuals will be saved for eternity.

Fantastic Changes!

Jesus will assume the throne that belongs to Him alone. It is called the "Throne of David." David, apparently, because of God's own choosing, will, in his supernatural state, also rule over the nation Israel during the Millennial era. "When the Son of man shall come in his glory, and all the holy angels with him, then shall he sit upon the throne of his glory" (Matt. 25:31). The terrain of Jerusalem, and the whole world will change in accordance with a masterful sweep of King Jesus' majestic hand.

We are given a glimpse of those astonishing topographical and environmental changes prophesied to take place in that day. (Read Isaiah 11:1-9 and Zechariah 14:4-9.)

Like in Eden

Jesus will make the earth like it was in the time of the Garden of Eden. It will be a crime-free world for the most part. Anyone who commits a crime will be dealt with immediately, and from a righteous justice system that has perfect knowledge of all things involved in the crime.

Many prophecy students believe Church Age saints will be officers of the Supreme Court of Justice in the administration of King Jesus. As supernatural officers of the Court, they will certainly be equipped to handle such a duty. But, crime will be almost non-existent, compared to our present hour. Christ's saints, both flesh and blood saints and supernatural saints, will doubtless have wonderfully creative things to do for those 1000 years. Anticipating that time of glorious service should empower us for our Royal Ambassador service here on earth!

For Additional Study

1. What are two mistakes those who are adamantly against the Pre-Trib view of Rapture make in most cases?

2. What are the two phases of Christ's Second coming?

3. What are the two groups of New Testament saints with which God will deal prophetically?

4. Give the Scripture for Satan's inability to overcome the saints of the Church Age.

5. Give the Scripture for Satan's being able to overcome the Tribulation saints.

6. Who are Christians told to look for—Jesus Christ, or Antichrist?

7. Are Christians told to look for the Tribulation, or for Jesus to take them home to Heaven?

8. Beside hosts of angels, who are in Christ's heavenly army as it descends to earth at Armageddon?

9. How will Christ slay the enemy armies that turn to attack the heavenly army?

10. Who will the goat nations be in the sheep/goat judgment?

11. Who will the Sheep nations be?

12. What will Church Age saints be doing during the millennial kingdom age?

God's Great Prophecy Power on Display

KEY PROPHECY POWER TRUTH

"And he that sat upon the throne said, Behold, I make all things new. And he said unto me, Write: for these words are true and faithful."

Revelation 21:5

Jesus Christ's 1000-year reign, called the "Millennial Kingdom," will come to a close with Satan's and mankind's final rebellion. God's prophetic Word says: "And when the thousand years are expired, Satan shall be loosed out of his prison, And shall go out to deceive the nations which are in the four quarters of the earth, Gog and Magog, to gather them together to battle: the number of whom is as the sand of the sea. And they went up on the breadth of the earth, and compassed the camp of the saints about, and the beloved city: and fire came down from God out of heaven, and devoured them" (Rev. 20:7-9).

Mankind Unchanged

Jesus has ruled by this time for a full 1000 years. The planet has been free of all demonic activity. Satan and his hordes are locked away—kept from any influence over human beings. The Lord has required everyone to live under His righteous rules, and earth has been almost without crime. Those who did break Millennial Law were quickly dealt with.

Despite the planet again being like Eden, with Jesus on the throne and Satan being locked in the bottomless pit, millions upon millions of people born during the 1000 years join Satan when he is released from the pit.

A Question of Proof

Why will God have the old serpent, the devil, released? Dr. J. Vernon McGee liked to quote Dr. Francis Schaefer, who McGee claimed said in answer to that question: "If you tell me why God turned him loose in the first place, I'll tell you why God turned him loose in the second place."

Probably, the short answer to why God will release Satan after the 1000 years have elapsed is that it will prove that man is still in the fallen state due to sin contamination in his genetic make-up.

Perhaps—even likely—the reason God will let Satan out of his bottomless pit jail cell is tied to why man, in spite of enjoying 1000 years of peace under the administration of the Prince of Peace, will rebel as did their ancestors down through pre-Millennial history.

They will surround Jerusalem to take Christ's throne. God will devour them all with fire. That will be the end of that.

Instant Judgment

No great battle—just, suddenly, the rebellion will be over. God's righteousness in dealing in judgment against sin and those who are sinful will be validated. The bloodstream of humanity at this point will still be contaminated by sin caused by the disobedience of the first man, Adam, in the Garden of Eden. The offspring of those who entered the millennial kingdom who haven't accepted Christ for their redemption will hate God and Christ, and will again fall for Satan's lies that they can become their own gods. The history of man, in the fallen, sin-filled flesh, will end then and there!

Satan Finished!

Satan and his angels will be thrown into the lake of fire. The Great White Throne Judgment will be held in the

Supreme court. All sin and lost sinners will be righteously judged, condemned and cast into the lake of fire.

Re-creation Power!

Then God will perform the astonishing act of re-creation of the heavens and the earth. His Omnipotence will discharge in an almighty display that will dissolve and remake all things, flashing across the eternal sphere with majesty, power, and glory!

The Great White Throne

Before the Lord makes all things new in the re-creation of the heavens and the earth, all the lost of all the ages must stand before Him at the Great White Throne. God's divine justice will at last righteously and forever deal with sin.

Worst Appointment Ever

Standing before the Great White Throne of God for judgment will be the worst appointment anyone will ever have to keep, except for the appointment that follows that judgment. The Scriptures report, in advance, that tragic time of hopelessness before the blazing, piercing holy eyes of God, the perfectly righteous Judge. "And I saw a great white throne, and him that sat on it, from whose face the earth and the heaven fled away; and there was found no place for them. And I saw the dead, small and great, stand before God; and the books were opened: and another book was opened, which is the book of life: and the dead were judged out of those things which were written in the books, according to their works. And the sea gave up the dead which were in it; and death and hell delivered up the dead which were in them: and they were judged every man according to their works" (Rev. 20:11-13).

Those who are summoned to be judged will know why they are there. They will have no excuses—no defense.

But, some will nonetheless plead the case they foolishly believe God will accept. "Not every one that saith unto me, Lord, Lord, shall enter into the kingdom of heaven; but he that doeth the will of my Father which is in heaven. Many will say to me in that day, Lord, Lord, have we not prophesied in thy name? and in thy name have cast out devils? and in thy name done many wonderful works? And then will I profess unto them, I never knew you: depart from me, ye that work iniquity" (Matt. 7:21-23).

Deadly Decision

Those who kneel before God at the Great White Throne will have, during physical life on earth, turned down the one person who could have kept them from this time of horror before this final court. They rejected Jesus Christ, who died to pay for their sins. If they would have just accepted His offer of forgiveness and salvation, they could have avoided this tragic moment. Jesus was their only Hope. He is the only advocate that stands before the Father. The Bible says: "For there is one God, and one mediator between God and men, the man Christ Jesus" (1 Tim. 2:5).

Self-Given Sentence

Everyone who is there for being judged is condemned already. The verdict is a foregone conclusion. It was decided at their physical death, before they were summoned. Each person appearing before the Great White Throne decided his own guilt, and his own punishment. And, his sentence is an eternal state of dying in the lake of fire. God's Word tells us: "And death and hell were cast into the lake of fire. This is the second death. And whosoever was not found written in the book of life was cast into the lake of fire" (Rev. 20:14, 15).

The Great White Throne Judgment awaits. That last and most horrific of all judgments from God will happen as surely as you are reading these words.

Unimaginable Fate

The worst torture by the worst diabolical dictators that have ever inflicted their terrors on other human beings will seem as nothing when compared to what awaits just beyond death apart from the True, Living God. Even Antichrist, who will perpetrate on people of the Tribulation a time of horror Jesus said will be the worst in human history, will come nowhere near producing the suffering that await those who stand before the Great White Throne.

Opposite the Bema

The Great White Throne Judgement will be, in every sense, the reverse of the Bema. The only thing the people of the two judgments will have in common is the fact that they will never die.

However, there is a profound difference in these two types of life without end. The saved who stand before the Judgement Seat of Christ will enter Heaven and experience living forever with ever-increasing exultation. The person who stands before the Great White Throne will enter into an eternity of dying without achieving death, while suffering ever-greater punishment and pain.

Just as the saved person will forever enjoy quality of life in Heaven based upon the rewards he has earned in physical life, so the person who is lost will spiral deeper into the torment of hell based upon the sins he committed in physical life.

Hell's Stark Reality

Realizing there are those, even among Bible-believing Christians, who will decry this treatment of the subject as barbaric, proclaiming that I've made God out to be a fiend, let us look at what His blessed Word has to say on the subject. Jesus' words present the stark reality of hell. The Lord says in the following verse: "And if thy foot offend thee, cut it off: it is better for thee to enter halt into life, than having two feet to be cast into hell, into the fire that never shall be quenched" (Mark 9:45).

Deserving Rebels

The Apostle Peter gives a precise description of the fate that awaits those who choose to ignore God's call to salvation through the sacrifice of His Son, Jesus, on the cross at Calvary. "For if God spared not the angels that sinned, but cast them down to hell, and delivered them into chains of darkness, to be reserved unto judgment; And spared not the old world, but saved Noah the eighth person, a preacher of righteousness, bringing in the flood upon the world of the ungodly; And turning the cities of Sodom and Gomorrah into ashes condemned them with an overthrow, making them an ensample unto those that after should live ungodly; And delivered just Lot, vexed with the filthy conversation of the wicked: (For that righteous man dwelling among them, in seeing and hearing, vexed his righteous soul from day to day with their unlawful deeds;) The Lord knoweth how to deliver the godly out of temptations, and to reserve the unjust unto the day of judgment to be punished: But chiefly them that walk after the flesh in the lust of uncleanness, and despise government. Presumptuous are they, self-willed, they are not afraid to speak evil of dignities. Whereas angels, which are greater in power and might, bring not railing accusation against them before the Lord. But these, as natural brute beasts, made to be taken and destroyed, speak evil of the things that they understand not; and shall utterly perish in their own corruption; And shall receive the reward of unrighteousness, as they that count it pleasure to riot in the day time. Spots they are and blemishes, sporting themselves with their own deceivings while they feast with you; Having eyes full of adultery, and that cannot cease from sin; beguiling unstable souls: an heart they have exercised with covetous practices; cursed children: Which have forsaken the right way, and are gone astray, following the way of Balaam the son of Bosor, who loved the wages of unrighteousness; But was rebuked for his iniquity: the dumb ass speaking with man's voice forbad the madness of the prophet. These are wells without water, clouds that are carried with a tempest; to whom the mist of darkness is reserved for ever" (2 Peter 2:4-17).

Some will say that Peter is talking about people of the worst sort, who are thus deserving of punishment. Peter, they will say, isn't talking about good people. However, it must be understood that all who haven't accepted Christ for salvation are considered unrighteous in God's holy eyes.

None Good

Jesus told the Truth of the matter: "And Jesus said unto him, Why callest thou me good? none is good, save one, that is, God" (Luke 18:19). The psalmist said: "Every one of them is gone back: they are altogether become filthy; there is none that doeth good, no, not one" (Psalm 53:3).

God sees those people who are not condemned to hell, only through His Son Jesus Christ. Christ's blood atonement for the remission of sin, thus for redemption of lost mankind, is the only hope for you and me. Without accepting God's offer of His Son for the saving of our souls, we are lost for eternity.

Fault Not God's

God throws no one into that indescribably terrible place of punishment called hell. He has done everything to make sure no one must go there. People put themselves in that place of torment forever when they reject the salvation Jesus Christ offers.

God's righteousness must deal with the thing called sin, therefore the Great White Throne awaits all who will not accept this grace gift from the God of Heaven who so loved the world that He gave His Son to die for all people.

Stunning Scientific Similarity

A recent news item sparked thoughts of this awful place called hell. Astronomers have discovered a black hole of dimension much larger than any they previously knew about. The scientists who study such things say that the black hole's gravity is so great, that it is literally tearing a gigantic star apart, and sucking it toward its center.

Black holes are mysterious entities in space where not even light can escape their hold. All things within the black hole's influence are tugged, and compacted into small configuration as the gravitational pull acts against them.

It is believed that even though there is no light, the heat is more intense within these black holes than is the temperature of stars.

One can't help thinking of such a place as being like the Bible's description of hell. Nothing and no one can escape. It is a place of total darkness and immense heat. hell is called "outer darkness" in a number of places.

Descriptions of hell imply total isolation, apart from God. The place called hell is implied to be the "sea of forgetfulness."

This means that God chooses to forget everything that is in that realm.

Can you imagine? God will not even remember those who choose to go to hell rather than accept His Son!

A Most Crucial Topic

Why spend so much space on the subject of the Great White Throne Judgment and hell? Because understanding in the deepest reaches of our souls the utter hopelessness and horrors that await those around us who are lost apart from Christ can generate great Holy Spirit-given desire within us, thus tremendous power to reach out with the Good News!

Greatest of All News!

The wonderful news—the Good News of the gospel—is that God is not willing that any should perish, but that all should have eternal life in Heaven with Him. Let us who name the name of Jesus urge the lost around us to accept Christ today. Let us pray they choose to listen to the Holy Spirit's call to their souls, so they, too, can look forward to the Bema rather than to the Great White Throne Judgment.

God's Creation Power Explodes

The black hole of outer darkness will swallow sin and hell itself. All evil will pass into the sea of forgetfulness forever. God, the Omnipotent, will step to the forefront of eternity. He will unleash divine creative power that will confound the infinite senses and dazzle the eyes of all the creatures within His limitless universes. God's powerful Prophetic Word says: "And I saw a new heaven and a new earth: for the first heaven and the first earth were passed away; and there was no more sea" (Rev. 21:1).

John, under divine inspiration, says further about God's astonishing re-creation: "And I John saw the holy city, new Jerusalem, coming down from God out of heaven, prepared as a bride adorned for her husband. And I heard a great voice out of heaven saying, Behold, the tabernacle of God is with men, and he will dwell with them, and they shall be his people, and God himself shall be with them, and be their God. And God shall wipe away all tears from their eyes; and there shall be no more death, neither sorrow, nor crying, neither shall there be any more pain: for the former things are passed away" (Rev. 21:2-4).

The Lord of Creation will cause the building blocks of the universes to fly apart. The very atoms will dissolve or melt with great heat, the temperature of which most likely never before was reached. The elements will pass into the ether of eternity with a hiss. The description given by some prophecy-oriented Bible scholars who understand the original language think the noise when the creation dissolves will sound like the lingering hiss that followed the nuclear bombs tested in the 1950s.

The Apostle Peter adds to our understanding of God's unfathomable act in the recreation of all things. In the following Scriptures he gives us the final scenes of old-earth history, beginning with the rapture (Christ's coming as a "thief in the night") and concluding with new heavens and a new earth, where God's perfect righteousness and peace abides for all eternity.

"But the day of the Lord will come as a thief in the night; in the which the heavens shall pass away with a great noise, and the elements shall melt with fervent heat, the earth also and the works that are therein shall be burned up. Seeing then that all these things shall be dissolved, what manner of persons ought ye to be in all holy conversation and godliness, Looking for and hasting unto the coming of the day of God, wherein the heavens being on fire shall be dissolved, and the elements shall melt with fervent heat? Nevertheless we, according to his promise, look for new heavens and a new earth, wherein dwelleth righteousness" (2 Peter 3:10-13).

We are then told how we are to conduct ourselves as God's children, while anticipating these stupendous prophetic events that will come to pass as surely as our Redeemer lives.

"Wherefore, beloved, seeing that ye look for such things, be diligent that ye may be found of him in peace, without spot, and blameless" (2 Peter 3:14).

Now, that's supernaturally inspired fuel for a prophecy-powered life!

For Additional Study

1. From where do the millions of people come, who join Satan in the final rebellion against God?

2. Why do these people rebel?

3. What will happen to these rebels?

4. What will happen to Satan?

5. Who will stand before the Great White Throne to be judged?

6. What happens to them after the judgment?

7. What is the one thing people who will be in hell, and people will be in Heaven will have in common?

8. Who causes people to have to be in hell for eternity?

9. What does the Christian's study about hell and its eternal consequences do for the believer?

10. What happens after all sin has been cast into the lake of fire?

The Prophecy Power-Filled Life

Part 1

KEY PROPHECY POWER TRUTH

"These things I have spoken unto you, that in me ye might have peace. In the world ye shall have tribulation: but be of good cheer; I have overcome the world."

John 16:33

This generation of Christians lives in times that are at once the most dangerous in history, and the most exciting. Our time on planet Earth is most dangerous, because in this late hour of human history Satan moves about ravenously desiring to see to it that every lost soul misses opportunities to accept the salvation message that is in Jesus Christ, alone. The Devil also wants to render ineffective the Christian's witness, and destroy the joy of our salvation. The Apostle Peter warns: "Be sober, be vigilant; because your adversary the devil, as a roaring lion, walketh about, seeking whom he may devour" (1 Peter 5:8).

An Exciting Time!

This is the most exciting time to be alive in history, because those who name the name of Jesus and watch expectantly for His appearing should be filled with Holy Spirit-given power and joy, knowing Christ can come at any moment.

The more we look at current issues and events, the more we will realize—if we are spiritually attuned to what God has put in His Word, the Bible—that Jesus' call "Come up hither!" (Rev. 4:1) must be near indeed. Again, the prophetic Word tells us: "And when these things begin to come to pass, then look up, and lift up your heads; for your redemption draweth nigh" (Luke 21:28).

A Power-Filled Life

Let's look in this lesson at the most pertinent of those issues and events that are beginning to come to pass. Then we will look in-depth, scripturally, at the crowns, or rewards, awaiting the Christian at the Judgment Seat of Christ, based upon service to our Lord while living here on earth.

Let's examine what God tells us about how to achieve, and live, a power-filled life, in part, by engaging in prayerful study of His prophetic Word.

The Prophecy Powered Life - Part One

The end-time battle for the souls of men and women, boys and girls, intensifies minute by minute. The struggle given so clearly in Scripture no longer takes place mostly in an unseen realm, where God's forces and Satan's forces clash in spiritual warfare, as we have learned from the following description. "For we wrestle not against flesh and blood, but against principalities, against powers, against the rulers of the darkness of this world, against spiritual wickedness in high places" (Eph. 6:12). The more the battle intensifies, let the words of Jesus empower you to fight on.

"These things I have spoken unto you, that in me ye might have peace. In the world ye shall have tribulation: but be of good cheer; I have overcome the world" (John 16:33).

Empowered for Battle

Now, the battle rages right in front of our eyes, and we are in the middle of it on a moment-by-moment level. Our news headlines every hour of every day report the battle, if we but examine the news in light of God's prophetic Word. When the Christian looks at what's going on all around us, with the prophetically biblical view, rather than the humanistic world-view, he is empowered through God's truth to understand the lateness of the hour and the crucial matters involved.

End-Time Issues and Events

Bible prophecy foretells specific issues and events that will take place at the end of the Church Age. The Church Age, as we have learned, is that era between the beginning of the church and the Rapture (the snatching up of believers from earth when Christ calls to take the saints back to Heaven where He has prepared mansions in His Father's House) (John 14:1-3).

Rapture Imminent

There are no prophecies that must be fulfilled before Christ raptures the saints. It is imminent—that is, it can happen at any moment. There are no signs to look for before the "twinkling of an eye" taking of saints into the air to meet Jesus. (Read 1 Corinthians 15:51-55, and 1 Thessalonians 4:13-18.) All prophetic signals given for the Second Coming of Christ were given for those who will endure the Tribulation (the last seven terrible years of human history also known as "Daniel's Seventieth Week").

However, even though God's prophetic Word didn't promise any signs to those who will be raptured, He is allowing us to see many foreshadowing signals that are setting the stage for the Tribulation. Specific signals prophesied to take place during the Tribulation are coming into view in our day.

Foreshadows of Apocalypse

If we see a person's shadow, we know he is there. Likewise, if we see the foreshadows of Antichrist, and the characteristics of the Tribulation, and of end-time man, we know those entities are in our immediate timeframe. The foreshadows of apocalypse are on our front pages. Therefore, since the Bible gives no signals to look for before the Rapture, and the Rapture will happen before the Tribulation begins, we are facing the glorious prospect of Rapture at any moment!

We will look first at the geopolitical arrangements that foreshadow the coming Tribulation. Next, we'll examine foreshadowing issues and events that look ominously like those prophesied by Jesus and the Old and New Testament prophets.

Geopolitical Foreshadows of Tribulation

Rearrangement of nations and geopolitical situations that have prophetic significance began in earnest early in the previous century. The rearrangements continue with astounding swiftness today.

• Russia and Islamic Nations

The Soviet Union, born in 1917 with the Bolshevik Revolution, became a stupendous military power by mid-century. The development of the atomic, then the hydrogen bombs, when combined with intercontinental ballistic missiles, made the USSR the most dangerous adversary to the U.S., and the peace of the world, on the planet. God raises up nations, and he brings them down. He so dealt with the Soviets, when in 1990, its empire came apart. That astonishes historians and geopolitical observers even today. The empire reduced to its original configuration and again became Russia. This is important to consider, when thinking on a major prophecy that will be fulfilled during the Tribulation.

The prophecy foretells: "And the word of the LORD came unto me, saying, Son of man, set thy face against Gog, the land of Magog, the chief prince of Meshech and Tubal, and prophesy against him, And say, Thus saith the Lord GOD; Behold, I am against thee, O Gog, the chief prince of Meshech and Tubal: And I will turn thee back, and put hooks into thy jaws, and I will bring thee forth, and all thine army, horses and horsemen, all of them clothed with all sorts of armour, even a great company with bucklers and shields, all of them handling swords. After many days thou shalt be visited: in the latter years thou shalt come into the land that is brought back from the sword, and is gathered out of many people, against the mountains of Israel, which have been always waste: but it is brought forth out of the nations, and they shall dwell safely all of them" (Ezek. 38:1-4, 8).

Gog-Magog Attack

This is the infamous Gog-Magog attack on Israel that is predicted before Christ's return at Armageddon. The leader is of the land of "Rosh," which is the ancient name for the area known today as Russia. The leader is called "Gog," and is "chief prince of Meshech and Tubal." "Meshech" is translated "Moscow" and "Tubal, "Tobalsk," modern-day Russian cities.

Space limitations prohibit a thorough study of the Gog-Magog attack on Israel. However, it is accurate to report that many prophetic scholars believe that Russia and the Islamic nations surrounding Russia that used to be part of the Soviet Union, with certain other nations of the region, seem to constitute the area from which will come the great force from the north that will attack Israel at some point. Some think the attack will take place just before the Tribulation begins. Others believe it will take place during the Tribulation, probably around the middle of the Tribulation period.

Point is, the Gog-Magog nations are in place. The stage for that prophesied event is set.

> This Gog-Magog attack must not be confused with the Gog-Magog attack led by Satan at the end of the millennial reign of Christ. They are two entirely different attacks.

• European Union

Jesus, shortly before He was crucified, gave the astonishing prophecy to His disciples while they sat together atop Mount Olivet overlooking the Temple. He said that the Temple would be torn apart. There wouldn't be a single stone upon another. Also, He said, Jerusalem would be savaged.

Jesus' prophecy came to pass in 70 A.D. Titus and the Roman army completely destroyed the Temple. Not one building block was left on another. Jerusalem was also laid ruin.

Daniel, centuries before that 70 A.D. event, prophesied: "And after threescore and two weeks shall Messiah be cut off, but not for himself: and the people of the prince that shall come shall destroy the city and the sanctuary; and the end

thereof shall be with a flood, and unto the end of the war desolations are determined" (Dan. 9:26).

Daniel foretold that the people of "the prince that shall
come," Antichrist, would destroy Jerusalem and the Temple.
It is the same prophecy Jesus gave in the Olivet Discourse.
The people of Antichrist were those within the Roman
Empire. The soldiers were Roman troops, led by Titus, the
Roman general. Daniel further prophesied: "And he shall confirm the covenant with many for one week: and in the midst
of the week he shall cause the sacrifice and the oblation to
cease, and for the overspreading of abominations he shall
make it desolate, even until the consummation, and that
determined shall be poured upon the desolate" (Dan. 9:27).

The Reviving Roman Empire

The Antichrist, Daniel foretold, will sign a covenant that
will ensure peace and safety with Israel and her neighbors,
and Israel's signing of that document will set in motion the
seven years of Tribulation. Although the Roman Empire fell
apart, it wasn't defeated. The prophecy foretold that the same
people would produce this end-time "prince"—Antichrist. The
European Union today is that reforming "people of the prince
that shall come." The EU is the reviving Roman Empire. It is
another strong geopolitical signal or foreshadowing that the
time of the Tribulation is very near.

• Israel

The Jewish people of Israel scattered from the region, from
the time of the 70 A.D. destruction of Jerusalem and the
Temple. They were persecuted in practically every nation to
which they fled for the next 1900-plus years. Many met horrible deaths, blamed for everything from killing Christ, to
causing the Black Plague.

They were people without a home, without a language,
without hope. Adolf Hitler tried to completely wipe them off
the earth, as have the radical Islamics since. Anti-Semitism
(hatred of Jews) is on the rise again in Europe and elsewhere.
It was and is satanic hatred, from the devil, and from the
degenerate hearts of man.

Israel seemed destined to the dustbin of history, never to rise again. But, God made a promise that Israel would be the head of the nations, and that He would never forsake them.

God Not Finished with Israel

Moses gave the Israelites this Word from their God. "For thou art an holy people unto the LORD thy God: the LORD thy God hath chosen thee to be a special people unto himself, above all people that are upon the face of the earth" (Deut. 7:6). David, king of Israel, said before God: "For thou hast confirmed to thyself thy people Israel to be a people unto thee for ever: and thou, LORD, art become their God" (2 Sam. 7:24).

The Old Testament prophets and Jesus foretold that the Jews would be scattered as a people. They were indeed scattered several times throughout history. The last scattering brings us to 1948.

Regathering Foretold

Just as many scatterings were foretold, so the Jews being regathered as a nation in the last days was foretold through prophecy. (I suggest that you read all of chapter 37 of Ezekiel to see God's regathering power regarding the last days for Israel.)

Israel was reborn in a single day, May 14, 1948. It is, in our day, becoming the greatest point of contention on the planet, so far as potential for triggering Armageddon is concerned. The prophet Zechariah foretold the situation as it would be at the end of the age, just before Christ's return. "The burden of the word of the LORD for Israel, saith the LORD, which stretcheth forth the heavens, and layeth the foundation of the earth, and formeth the spirit of man within him. Behold, I will make Jerusalem a cup of trembling unto all the people round about, when they shall be in the siege both against Judah and against Jerusalem. And in that day will I make Jerusalem a burdensome stone for all people: all that burden themselves with it shall be cut in pieces, though all the people of the earth be gathered together against it" (Zech. 12:1-3).

Israel is the most profound geopolitical foreshadowing of the looming Tribulation.

Issues and Events That Foreshadow Tribulation

We live today in times marked by issues and events like those prophesied for the last days. There are too many such issues and events to deal with in this limited space. Let's look at just a few.

• Without Natural Affection

Homosexuality, a sinful, perverted existence that leads to disease and death is called "gay life-style." Babies are killed while in their mother's wombs, usually for the sake of convenience. These two issues, even if considered without adding others, make up an end-time characteristic the Apostle Paul forewarned will mark the last days. Paul said: "This know also, that in the last days perilous times shall come. For men shall be . . . without natural affection" (2 Tim. 3:1-3).

Can it be "natural affection" when people of the same sex engage in sexual activity together? Can it be "natural affection" that rips a baby from a mother's womb because the child would be an inconvenience? Many other "unnatural" activities spin from the collective mind-set that holds that homosexuality should be called "gay," and abortion is an acceptable—even preferable, form of birth control.

We are familiar with the problems within organizations in which young boys are involved, such as Boy Scouts. The news stories have revealed the predators who take advantage as leaders of troops. The writers of the news, most of which are liberal-minded journalists that champion "gay rights issues" won't portray the growing problem within the Scouts and other such organizations as a homosexual problem. They most often want it to be seen as a pedophile problem. It is both.

Recent stories abound about Catholic clergy involved in gross immorality, much of the problem involving homosexual predators preying on young boys. More and more we get reports of young mothers aborting babies, or leaving just-born infants in places like restrooms, or even garbage cans. We read and hear stories of mothers killing their children because they've become inconvenient to relationships with boyfriends. "Without natural affection" seems to describe our times accurately.

• Fierce . . . Despisers of Those That Are Good

We have looked briefly before at these characteristics of end-time man as outlined by Paul the apostle in 2 Timothy, chapter 3. Another look is in order here, because there are no stronger indicators of where we stand on God's prophetic timeline than those Paul calls "fierce" and "despisers of those that are good."

The Columbine, Colorado horror of a few years ago sums up both of these end-time symptoms in one heartbreaking story. The teen-age boys who murdered classmates chose in particular a group of Christian young people on whom to concentrate their murderous rage. Remember the girl they shot in the face after she refused to agree to their demand to renounce her faith in God?

The growing hatred for those in America who want to be guided by the Bible-based moral compass set in place by our founding fathers is clear indication that there are forces in this nation that are "despisers of those that are good" (those who hold to godly principles).

Prophecy Power for Godly Living

We are commanded to live godly lives, despite opposition that's predicted to grow as time of the end of the age approaches. Paul tells us: "Yea, and all that will live godly in Christ Jesus shall suffer persecution" (2 Tim. 3:12).

Won't Regret Obedience

Our obedience will be worth the troubles of this life, however. And, that's a real understatement! Our rewards for living as our Lord wants us to live while under such persecution will be beyond our wildest imaginations. Crowns of victory will be given at the Bema (Judgment Seat of Christ) that will make everything we might have endured in life fade to nothingness.

Paul wrote, expounding upon Isaiah 64:4: "But as it is written, Eye hath not seen, nor ear heard, neither have entered into the heart of man, the things which God hath prepared for them that love him" (1 Cor. 2:9). Let's look, under scriptural examination, at the crowns Christians will receive at the Bema.

Great Rewards Await!
The Bible mentions at least five crowns/rewards.

1. The Incorruptible Crown—Given to those who master the old nature:

"And every man that striveth for the mastery is temperate in all things. Now they do it to obtain a corruptible crown; but we an incorruptible. I therefore so run, not as uncertainly; so fight I, not as one that beateth the air: But I keep under my body, and bring it into subjection: lest that by any means, when I have preached to others, I myself should be a castaway" (1 Cor. 9:25-27).

2. The Crown of Rejoicing—Given to soul winners:

"For what is our hope, or joy, or crown of rejoicing? Are not even ye in the presence of our Lord Jesus Christ at his coming? For ye are our glory and joy" (1 Thess. 2:19, 20).

"The fruit of the righteous is a tree of life; and he that winneth souls is wise" (Prov. 11:30).

(See also: Daniel 12:31.)

3. The Crown of Life—Given to those who successfully endure temptation:

"My brethren, count it all joy when ye fall into divers temptations; Knowing this, that the trying of your faith worketh patience" (James 1:2, 3).

"Fear none of those things which thou shalt suffer: behold, the devil shall cast some of you into prison, that ye may be tried; and ye shall have tribulation ten days: be thou faithful unto death, and I will give thee a crown of life" (Rev. 2:10).

4. The Crown of Righteousness—Given to those who especially love the doctrine of the Rapture:

"Henceforth there is laid up for me a crown of righteousness, which the Lord, the righteous judge, shall give me at that day: and not to me only, but unto all them also that love his appearing" (2 Tim. 4:8).

5. The Crown of Glory—Given to faithful preachers and teachers:

"Feed the flock of God which is among you, taking the oversight thereof, not by constraint, but willingly; not for filthy lucre, but of a ready mind; Neither as being lords over God's heritage, but being ensamples to the flock. And when the chief Shepherd shall appear, ye shall receive a crown of glory that fadeth not away" (1 Peter 5:2-4).

(See also: Acts 20:26-28; 2 Timothy 4:1, 2.)

Keeping in mind that we strive for crowns with which to honor our Lord, let us be empowered by the promise of God's prophetic Word!

For Additional Study

1. Why is ours the most dangerous time in human history?

2. Why is ours the most exciting time in human history?

3. What are we as Christians supposed to do while we witness end-time events?

4. Who is it the Bible tells us are our primary enemies?

5. How can we be victorious over these satanic forces?

6. The signs given by Jesus and the prophets were foretelling what era of human history?

7. Why, then, are we, who are in the Church Age, seeing these Tribulation era issues and events?

8. Give 3 geo-political foreshadowings of the coming Tribulation.

9. Give two issues in our time that meet the definition of the Apostle Paul's last-days, perilous-times symptoms (2 Timothy, chapter 3).

10. What does the prophetic Word have to say about saints who endure these times, and live for Christ victoriously?

The Prophecy Power-Filled Life

Part 2

KEY PROPHECY POWER TRUTH

"And, behold, I come quickly; and my reward is with me, to give every man according as his work shall be."

Revelation 22:12

Our final session will investigate, through in-depth scriptural analysis, everything about what it takes to live the power-filled life. Prophecy is at the heart of our investigation, because there are certain areas given by God's Word that we, as God's children, will be tested on when we stand before Jesus at the prophesied Bema (Judgment Seat of Christ).

[Editors note: I would like here to express my profound thanks to Dr. H. L. Wilmington for his prayerfully considered faithfulness to God's Word in putting together the following study of areas of life in which each believer in Jesus Christ will be examined at the Bema. Also, I give him my thanks for giving me permission to use it as I see fit. Dr. Wilmington, who is a professor at Liberty University, Lynchburg, Virginia, compiled the list of areas in which Christians will be tested, with the Scriptures. The commentary beneath each area is mine. –TJ]

Now, let's get started on an adventure into learning specific areas and activities in which the Lord expects us to excel as His Royal Ambassadors in His Majesty's service while we live the hours, days, weeks, months and years He has given us in this life.

Bema Areas for Testing

Dr. H.L. Wilmington has done a good job of gleaning the truth about the things upon which Christians will be examined at the Judgment Seat of Christ. They are as follows:

1. How we treat other believers

- "For God is not unrighteous to forget your work and labour of love, which ye have shewed toward his name, in that ye have ministered to the saints, and do minister" (Heb. 6:10).
- "He that receiveth a prophet in the name of a prophet shall receive a prophet's reward; and he that receiveth a righteous man in the name of a righteous man shall receive a righteous man's reward. And whosoever shall give to drink unto one of these little ones a cup of cold water only in the name of a disciple, verily I say unto you, he shall in no wise lose his reward" (Matt. 10:41, 42).

Disagreement between Christians can be among the most hurtful. God tells us through His Word that we will judge angels. We must be very careful with judging fellow believers, because they, too, are very highly placed in the Lord's prophetic plans. There are biblical prescriptions for dealing with a hurting, and/or fallen brother and sister, but nowhere are we told to deal in anger or hatred. We should do everything possible to direct those who need help to the Lord, and to lift them up ourselves whenever possible. Apparently, how we treat our fellow Christians sits atop the list of the works for which we will be tested at the Judgment Seat of Christ.

2. How we exercise our authority over others

- "Obey them that have the rule over you, and submit yourselves: for they watch for your souls, as they that must give account, that they may do it with joy, and not with grief: for that is unprofitable for you" (Heb. 13:17).

- "My brethren, be not many masters, knowing that we shall receive the greater condemnation" (James 3:1).

It has been said that some people grow in authority. We sometimes have seen this in presidents. Harry S. Truman, who wasn't even called in for consultation with President Roosevelt during Truman's vice presidency, was suddenly thrust into the middle of crucial World War II planning and decision-making when Roosevelt died. By all accounts, this short, unassuming man from a small town in Missouri grew immensely in his role as president. He exercised his authority well, by most accounts, and the war was won against Hitler and the empire of Japan.

While some grow with authority, however, others just swell. They become puffed-up. God takes a dim view of self-pride. Think about it. This was the thing that brought the great Lucifer down. It is the temptation to which Adam and Eve fell. Let us think more of others than of ourselves. This is the attitude that will most please Jesus while we work toward our Bema appointment with Him.

3. How we employ our God-given abilities

- "Now there are diversities of gifts, but the same Spirit. For as the body is one, and hath many members, and all the members of that one body, being many, are one body: so also is Christ" (1 Cor. 12:4, 12).
- "Wherefore I put thee in remembrance that thou stir up the gift of God, which is in thee by the putting on of my hands" (2 Tim. 1:6).
- "As every man hath received the gift, even so minister the same one to another, as good stewards of the manifold grace of God" (1 Peter 4:10).
- Read also Jesus' teaching of the Parables of the ten pounds (Luke 19:11-26) and the talents (Matt. 25:14-29).

Each believer has at least one talent. (See 1 Corinthians 7:7; 12:7-11; Ephesians 4:7; 1 Peter 4:10; study Romans 12; 1 Corinthians 12; Ephesians 4.) It's up to each believer to find/discern his God-given abilities. Others can often see those talents in us before we do. It is vital to use our abilities, not to aggrandize ourselves, but to benefit the body of Christ, and to reach out to those who don't know Christ as Savior. Many lose the effectiveness or potential of their talents at some points in their lives, if they deliberately and continually refuse to use them the way God desires. Sadly, those who haven't employed their gifts for God's work on earth will not receive rewards at the Bema that would have otherwise been theirs.

4. How we use our money

- "Upon the first day of the week let every one of you lay by him in store, as God hath prospered him, that there be no gatherings when I come" (1 Cor. 16:2).

- "But this I say, He which soweth sparingly shall reap also sparingly; and he which soweth bountifully shall reap also bountifully. Every man according as he purposeth in his heart, so let him give; not grudgingly, or of necessity: for God loveth a cheerful giver" (2 Cor. 9:6, 7).

- "Charge them that are rich in this world, that they be not highminded, nor trust in uncertain riches, but in the living God, who giveth us richly all things to enjoy; That they do good, that they be rich in good works, ready to distribute, willing to communicate; Laying up in store for themselves a good foundation against the time to come, that they may lay hold on eternal life" (1 Tim. 6:17-19).

- All belongs to God: "Forasmuch as ye know that ye were not redeemed with corruptible things, as silver and gold, from your vain conversation received by tradition from your fathers; But with the precious blood of Christ, as of a lamb without blemish and without spot" (1 Peter 1:18, 19).

Each of us has a different level of income and money to tithe and give to God's work. But, the amount we can give means nothing in God's eternal economy. That we give cheerfully, with desire to obey and please God . . . that's what concerns Him. Remember the widow's two mites. She gave all she had. Jesus was most pleased in pointing that out to those He was teaching. Undoubtedly that widow will have a tremendous heavenly reward. But, I believe it's safe to consider that God took care of her earthly needs at every crisis in her life, as well.

We leave our earthly bank accounts behind; we go to our heavenly bank accounts. The earthly is but a few years; we will draw on the heavenly for all eternity.

5. How we spend our time

- "So teach us to number our days, that we may apply our hearts unto wisdom" (Psalm 90:12).
- "Redeeming the time, because the days are evil" (Eph. 5:16).
- "Walk in wisdom toward them that are without, redeeming the time" (Col. 4:5).
- "And if ye call on the Father, who without respect of persons judgeth according to every man's work, pass the time of your sojourning here in fear" (1 Peter 1:17).

Slothfulness is a sin that God warns against. His children are expected to be busy here on this fallen planet. We are His royal ambassadors, and there is much to be done. This means we should be active for our Lord while we go about our daily lives. It doesn't mean we are expected to spend every waking moment in prayer, Bible reading, or church attendance. We are, however, to do these things in their order, and to live every moment before the unsaved as a child of God. We are to be light and salt to a dark, sin-decaying world.

We all have different amounts of money to give to the Lord's work. Whether we spend that money differs with each person. In the matter of time, every person begins each week with 168 hours. Each of us will spend every hour of that time. How we spend it, whether with obedience to God in our hearts and minds, or on other things, will determine the rewards we receive at the Bema.

6. How much we suffer for Jesus

- "Blessed are ye, when men shall revile you, and persecute you, and shall say all manner of evil against you falsely, for my sake. Rejoice, and be exceeding glad: for great is your reward in heaven: for so persecuted they the prophets which were before you" (Matt. 5:11, 12).

- "And Jesus answered and said, Verily I say unto you, There is no man that hath left house, or brethren, or sisters, or father, or mother, or wife, or children, or lands, for my sake, and the gospel's, But he shall receive an hundredfold now in this time, houses, and brethren, and sisters, and mothers, and children, and lands, with persecutions; and in the world to come eternal life" (Mark 10:29, 30).

- "For I reckon that the sufferings of this present time are not worthy to be compared with the glory which shall be revealed in us" (Rom. 8:18).

- "For our light affliction, which is but for a moment, worketh for us a far more exceeding and eternal weight of glory" (2 Cor. 4:17).

- "Beloved, think it not strange concerning the fiery trial which is to try you, as though some strange thing happened unto you: But rejoice, inasmuch as ye are partakers of Christ's sufferings; that, when his glory shall be revealed, ye may be glad also with exceeding joy" (1 Peter 4:12, 13).

It is interesting that many who promote the "prosperity" message that God will bless the giver with great material wealth when a person gives to their particular ministry, never mention the hundredfold blessings promised in the Scriptures above. Those blessings come at the cost of suffering for Christ in this life. That is not a message that appeals to many. Prosperity preachers and teachers especially don't seem interested in sermonizing on the prophetic promise that those who suffer for Jesus in this life will receive great heavenly rewards.

Many Christians want to grasp onto the power in the first part of Philippians 3:10, which reads: "That I may know him, and the power of his resurrection." But, they rarely want to adopt the second part of that verse as their life's motto. It reads: "And the fellowship of his sufferings, being made conformable unto his death."

Let us, like the Apostle Paul, know how both to abound, and how to suffer for Christ, desiring that in all things, He receives the preeminence. Let us diminish, like John the Baptist wanted to do, so that Jesus is lifted higher, in order that the lost world will be drawn to Him for salvation.

Great rewards await Christians willing to suffer for Jesus.

7. How we run that particular race God has chosen for us

- "Know ye not that they which run in a race run all, but one receiveth the prize? So run, that ye may obtain" (1 Cor. 9:24).
- "Holding forth the word of life; that I may rejoice in the day of Christ, that I have not run in vain, neither laboured in vain" (Phil. 2:16).
- "Brethren, I count not myself to have apprehended: but this one thing I do, forgetting those things which are behind, and reaching forth unto those things which are before, I press toward the mark for the prize of the high calling of God in Christ Jesus" (Phil. 3:13, 14).
- "Wherefore seeing we also are compassed about with so great a cloud of witnesses, let us lay aside every weight, and the sin which doth so easily beset us, and let us run with patience the race that is set before us" (Heb. 12:1).

Paul's example was a great one. How we run the race of life will determine whether we hear Jesus' words "Well done, good, faithful servant." That will be reward enough!

8. How effectively we control the old nature

- "And every man that striveth for the mastery is temperate in all things. Now they do it to obtain a corruptible crown; but we an incorruptible. I therefore so run, not as uncertainly; so fight I, not as one that beateth the air: But I keep under my body, and bring it into subjection: lest that by any means, when I have preached to others, I myself should be a castaway" (1 Cor. 9:25-27).

Paul used the Greek word adokimos when indicating disapproval of self. To "castaway" is the meaning. Paul wanted to keep his old nature in check—seen in the following Scriptures:

- "Study to shew thyself approved unto God, a workman that needeth not to be ashamed, rightly dividing the word of truth" (2 Tim. 2:15).
- "That ye may approve things that are excellent; that ye may be sincere and without offence till the day of Christ" (Phil. 1:10).
- "But as we were allowed of God to be put in trust with the gospel, even so we speak; not as pleasing men, but God, which trieth our hearts" (1 Thess. 2:4).

Keeping the old nature in check is a difficult thing that can't be done apart from help from the Holy Spirit. First, however, we must want to do so in our desire to serve the Lord. Let us, minute-by-minute seek God's help in bringing our self-will into subjection to His will.

9. How many souls we witness to, and win to Christ

- "The fruit of the righteous is a tree of life; and he that winneth souls is wise" (Prov. 11:30).
- "And they that be wise shall shine as the brightness of the firmament; and they that turn many to righteousness as the stars for ever and ever" (Dan. 12:3).
- "For what is our hope, or joy, or crown of rejoicing? Are not even ye in the presence of our Lord Jesus Christ at his coming? For ye are our glory and joy" (1 Thess. 2:19, 20).

God's foremost priority is saving the lost from sin. As a matter of fact, God loves lost people so much He sent His Son, Jesus, to die for them. Should we who name the name of Jesus have as our top priority any less a goal, than to help lost souls come to a saving knowledge of our Lord? Our desire and our efforts to win the lost to Christ will determine our rewards when we face Jesus at the Bema.

10. How we react to temptation

- "My brethren, count it all joy when ye fall into divers temptations; Knowing this, that the trying of your faith worketh patience" (James 1:2, 3).

- "Because thou hast kept the word of my patience, I also will keep thee from the hour of temptation, which shall come upon all the world, to try them that dwell upon the earth" (Rev. 3:10).

Today, we, especially in America, face temptations the intensity of which is greater than those faced by any other generation. We are bombarded every minute of everyday with ways to distract us from God and His work. Jesus, however, said there is no temptation we face that He didn't face—and overcome.

We who are Christians are promised to be kept out of the ultimate hour of temptation—the Tribulation era. Then, people will be tempted to take the Antichrist's mark, or die. Now, that will be a terrible temptation!

Jesus has crowns of great eternal value awaiting those who choose Him, and His all-important work on earth, rather than the temporary thrills and seductions offered by Satan and the present world-system.

11. How much the doctrine of the Rapture means to us
- "Henceforth there is laid up for me a crown of righteousness, which the Lord, the righteous judge, shall give me at that day: and not to me only, but unto all them also that love his appearing" (2 Tim. 4:8).

Are you looking for the any-moment call from Jesus, "Come up hither"? Paul prophesies a "twinkling of an eye" experience in which Christians will vanish from the planet's surface to be forever with their Savior and Lord, Jesus.

Paul foretells, further, of a "crown of righteousness" for those who are truly desiring Jesus' appearing to take them to Heaven. Therefore, we can know that the study of Bible prophecy, and the doctrine of the Rapture must be all-important to the Lord.

12. How faithful we are to the Word of God, and the flock of God
- "Wherefore I take you to record this day, that I am pure from the blood of all men. For I have not shunned to

declare unto you all the counsel of God. Take heed therefore unto yourselves, and to all the flock, over the which the Holy Ghost hath made you overseers, to feed the church of God, which he hath purchased with his own blood" (Acts 20:26-28).

- "I charge thee therefore before God, and the Lord Jesus Christ, who shall judge the quick and the dead at his appearing and his kingdom; Preach the word; be instant in season, out of season; reprove, rebuke, exhort with all longsuffering and doctrine" (2 Tim. 4:1, 2).
- "Feed the flock of God which is among you, taking the oversight thereof, not by constraint, but willingly; not for filthy lucre, but of a ready mind; Neither as being lords over God's heritage, but being ensamples to the flock. And when the chief Shepherd shall appear, ye shall receive a crown of glory that fadeth not away" (1 Peter 5:2-4).

We must handle the Word of God faithfully, proclaiming its power and truth to all the world. There must be no deceit involved in giving out the word; we can't just pick and choose verses out of context to fit our opinion. We must pray and meditate upon the Word, for the Word is in actuality, a Person—the Word is Jesus!

Those who preach and teach the Word in the right way are promised a crown of glory. Truly believing this and all other prophetic promises empowers the Christian's life every moment of every day.

For Additional Study

1. List as many of the areas in which Christians will be examined as you can. Give your thoughts—in diary, or journal fashion—on each area, for helping your future growth as a saint of God.

Let these areas of life be subjects of a diary, or journal while you study and apply the scriptural principles involved under each heading.

Answers to For Additional Study Questions

Lesson 1
1. Jesus
2. Empower Christians for their missions
3. Know the enemy
4. The Bible
5. About 27%
6. Forthtelling; Foretelling
7. Forthtelling: Speaking with Holy Spirit discernment about current issues and events
   Forthtelling: Inspired revelation; telling with 100% accuracy what will happen in the future
8. 1) So we will not be ignorant of God's program in the future
   2) Because God wants us to know His prophetic plan
   3) In order that we comfort and encourage each other that, for us, history has a joyous ending
   4) Because Bible prophecy will challenge us to live godly lives

Lesson 2
1. In a time we think not.
2. The days of Noah and of Lot
3. Business and life were going along normally. There was much violence upon the whole earth.
4. None.
5. 1) Take away the fear, gloom and doom of the future;
   2) The student of Bible prophecy is given Holy Spirit understanding that God's is the correct worldview, and the humanistic worldview is wrong
6. 1) Living godly lives, desiring the coming of the Lord
   2) Be blameless, and in peace, before the world around us (2 Peter 3:11-14)
7. The beginning of God's dealing with man from the time of Rapture, until the remaking of the heavens and earth.
8. 21
9. To fully realize their severity, so we will desire to see the lost come to Christ in order for them to avoid having to endure the coming judgments.
10. 1 Thessalonians 5:9-11
11. 1) The Rapture (His coming in the air for the saints)
    2) The Second Advent (coming all the way to earth)

Lesson 3
1. 2 Peter 3:3, 4
2. Evolutionary scientists have never been able to find even one authentic fossil as example that one specie has made the sudden leap to another. There are no links of one specie to another.
3. Satan

150

4. "The spirit of Antichrist" (1 John 4:1-3)
5. No!
6. 2 Samuel 7:24
7. Jesus Christ is the power of God's love. That powerful love produces in the individual Christian the desire to sow the seed of the Gospel message that Jesus saves!
8. That false teachers will try to delude and seduce even true believers in order to satisfy their own covetous desires. This kind of activity today is a definite signal we are in the last time.
9. Bible prophecy forewarns about such seductive persons. The student of prophecy will gain wisdom to spot them, and resist their allure.

Lesson 4
1. 2 Timothy 3:1-5
2. How about road rage?
3. Porn on the Internet, prescription pain-killers, cocaine
4. Abortion, homosexuality
5. "Thou shall have no other gods before me."
6. "Our God is one Lord: And thou shalt love the Lord thy God with all thy heart, and with all thy soul, and with all thy mind, and with all thy strength: this is the first commandment" (Mark 12:28-30).
7. "And when these things begin to come to pass, then look up, and lift up your heads; for your redemption draweth nigh" (Luke 21:28).
8. Low self-esteem
9. Self-love

Lesson 5
1. Everything.
2. 1 Thessalonians 4:13-18 and 1 Corinthians 15:51-55
3. Their bodies will be changed into supernatural bodies. They will vanish from earth, and appear instantly before Christ above the earth.
4. They will be changed into supernatural bodies that then will join to their souls. They, too, will appear instantly before Christ in the air above earth.
5. Forever!
6. All who have accepted Christ as Savior, both the living, and those who have died.
7. Back to the Father's House—Heaven.
8. John 14:1-3
9. The study of end-time matters.
10. Daniel 12:4
11. 1) Split Rapture; 2) Mid-Trib Rapture; 3) Post-Trib Rapture; 4) Pre-Trib Rapture

Lesson 6
1. Sin.
2. The Return of Jesus Christ.
3. The man of sin—Antichrist

4. The Holy Spirit, resident within the saints.
5. The signals He gave will come with greater frequency and intensity, like the pains of a woman in labor.
6. The days of Noah, and the days of Lot.
7. Israel back in a part of its promised land, and involved in turmoil, with the peace process at the center of it all.
8. Humanism is man (people) doing things their own way, apart from God. And, that what's wrong with it. The end of it is a downward moral slide to death.
9. He will take his governing hand off for a time, and let man have it his way. The result will be a quick degeneration into complete chaos.

Lesson 7

1. Jesus Christ
2. To examine the lives of saints to determine eternal rewards
3. No. Jesus forever took sin guilt away on the cross for all whom believe.
4. 1) The Bema Judgment: For those who are saved, only. This Judgment takes place first.
   2) The Great White Throne Judgment: This is for the lost, only. It will take place at the end of Christ's 1000-year reign on earth.
5. Ourselves. We are to do our very best in service to Christ, with what talents God has given us.
6. The Olympic games, with the judges' raised podium (the Bema) for handing out victory wreaths.
7. Jesus Christ, the Son of the Living God.
8. He is called "the chief corner stone." He is prophesied to be the stone "made without hands" that smashes the man-image of Babylonian King Nebuchadnezzar's dream-vision on the feet in Daniel, chapter 2.
9. We are to build upon it with our works for His honor and glory. Upon the building materials we use, will depend the opulent quality of our eternal life in Heaven.
10. gold, silver, precious stones, wood hay, stubble
11. To hear our Lord Jesus say: "Well done, thy good and faithful servant."
12. We will cast the crowns at Jesus' feet, in acknowledgment that He, alone, is worthy of all honor and glory.

Lesson 8

1. Noah's Flood
2. During the Tribulation era, the last seven years of this earth age.
3. 21 specific judgments in a series of 7 scroll, 7 trumpet, and 7 vial (bowl) judgments
4. Yes. Antichrist will bring about peace. But it will be false peace, that God's Word says will "destroy many" (Daniel 8:25).
5. Israel's agreeing to the covenant of peace that Antichrist guarantees
6. Daniel 9:26, 27
7. 1) To purge out a remnant of Israel that will accept Christ as Messiah;

2) to save a vast number of Gentiles out of that era who will accept Christ as Savior.

8. (See list near end of Lesson 8)

9. At least one-half of the world's population.

Lesson 9

1. Because God is outside of the timeline He created for man and earth history.

2. Because the 24 Elders, some of whom must be the saints of the Church Age, are seated around the Throne observing Jesus' opening the seals.

3. Jesus Christ—The "Lamb of God"

4. From the unsealing of the first seal in Revelation 6:1. All of the 7 seals represent God's judgment (Revelation 6:17).

5. White, Red, Black, Chloros (or pale)

6. White horse rider represents false peace; Red horse rider represents war; Black horse rider represents pestilence and famine; Pale horse rider represents death, with a second rider representing hell.

7. About one-fourth of the world's population.

8. Rather than repent, they will curse God, the Bible says.

9. 100-pound hailstones, and an earthquake, the greatest in history, that flattens every city on earth.

Lesson 10

1. 1) They see one Second Coming, not one Second Coming in two phases.
   2) They see God as having one prophetic program only –for all saints, not two groups of saints.

2. 1) The Return in the Rapture; 2) The coming back to earth for His Millennial Reign

3. 1) Those of the Church Age
   2) Those of the Tribulation era

4. Matthew 16:18

5. Revelation 13:7

6. Jesus Christ (Titus 2:13)

7. Jesus to take them home to Heaven (John 14:1-3)

8. All saints

9. With the power of His word, likened to a sword.

10. All nations that have dealt unkindly with Israel

11. All nations who have dealt kindly with Israel.

12. Rule and reign with King Jesus.

Lesson 11

1. They are offspring of the saints who survived the Tribulation to repopulate the Millennial earth.

2. Because they reject Christ, like all other rebels against God. They still have the sin-contaminated bloodline from Adam's original sin.

3. They will be consumed by heavenly fire, then cast into outer darkness.

4. This time he and all his angels will be cast into the lake of fire where he will be tormented day and night forever, along with the Antichrist and false prophet, who will have been there for 1000 years already.

5. All the lost (those who have rejected salvation through Christ) throughout all of human history.

6. All are cast into the lake of fire for eternity.

7. Neither will die. Those in hell will be in an eternal state of dying, but death can't come. People in Heaven will live lives that get better and better, forever.

8 The person himself, by refusing his only hope for salvation—Jesus Christ. God places no one there. Sinners put themselves in the lake of fire forever.

9. It should create in each the fervent desire to lift Jesus up before the lost, so people will see Him as their only Hope, when the Holy Spirit convicts (calls) them to believe in Christ.

10. God remakes the heavens and the earth with a consuming, and at the same time, creative fire. The heavenly city, Jerusalem, then descends from Heaven to be a part of the new Earth.

Lesson 12

1. Because Satan seeks to destroy, and realizes time is short for him to do his destructive work.

2. Because we are a part of the wind-up to the end of the age, when Jesus will Rapture believers to be with Him forever.

3. We are to look up, because Jesus is about to call us to be with Him (Luke 21:28).

4. Powers, principalities, and wickedness in high (supernatural) places (Ephesians 6:12).

5. By putting on the whole armor of God, and depending upon Jesus, who has already overcome all of them (John 16:33).

6. The Tribulation (last seven years before Jesus comes back at the Second Advent).

7. We are not in the Tribulation era. God, in His grace and love, is allowing us to see the signs given by Jesus and the prophets develop, so we are forewarned of the rapidly approaching apocalyptic storm.

8. 1) The Gog-Magog forces (probably Russia, and many Islamic nations surrounding Israel) are in place for a the future attack on Israel predicted in Ezekiel 38 and 39.

2) The European Union seems to be the reviving Roman Empire, which was the 4th great world empire foretold by Daniel the prophet to come upon the earth, is gaining strength. It is the region out of which Antichrist will come.

3) Israel is at the center of world controversy, after being scattered as a people for centuries. They have their common language again, and there is a peace process that may lead to the false peace of Daniel 9:27.

9. The symptom "without natural affection" is perhaps the best example. In our day homosexuality, and abortion mark this as, most likely, the last-days generation.
10. The Apostle Paul wrote, expounding upon Isaiah's prophecy, that it's beyond our imagination, the fantastic rewards God has prepared for those who love Him (1 Corinthians 2:9).

Lesson 13
Let these areas of life be subjects of a diary, or journal while you study and apply the scriptural principles involved under each heading.